# Strive for M.O.R.E.
What wellbeing really means & how you can achieve it.

**Jan Raedar – The Selfcare Sensei**

This Certificate issued under the seal of the Copyright Office in accordance with title 17, United States Code, attests that registration has been made for the work identified below. The information on this certificate has been made a part of the Copyright Office records.

*Shira Perlmutter*

United States Register of Copyrights and Director

Registration Number

**TXu 2-396-665**

**Effective Date of Registration:**
October 04, 2023
**Registration Decision Date:**
November 06, 2023

# Title

**Title of Work:** Strive for M.O.R.E.: What wellbeing really means & how you can achieve it

# Completion/Publication

Year of Completion: 2023

# Author

**Author:** Janice Raeder

**Author Created:** text

**Work made for hire:** No

**Citizen of:** United States

*For all of those who shared your story with me, I'm truly honored. I learned so much from your struggles and your triumphs. Without you, I would not have been inspired to write this book.*

*To the reader, thank you for giving my words a chance.*

# ACKNOWLEDGMENT

This is the part of this book where I get to practice gratitude. Something that we will talk about many times in the pages to follow.

First and foremost, this labor of love would not have been possible without the support of my soulmate, William Reid. Thank you for your patience each time I read portions of this book to you. Sometimes, it was a chore for you to listen, but you never let on!

I would also like to shout out to my nephew, Jonathan Bull. You were so generous with your time and your feedback. I am truly grateful.

Chelsea Fincham, your suggestions and support during this project were invaluable. Thanks for being one of my biggest cheerleaders!

I would also like to include Cindy Bates, Anastasia Pratt, Sylvain Nagler, and Cathy Davison. Thank you all for your guidance and support when I returned to higher education. You taught me so much about the breadth and depth of higher learning.

I would be remiss if I did not acknowledge all the students and parents at US Budokai Karate. Being a small part of your "a-ha" moments is the greatest gift one could ever receive. You all have helped shape the way I live my life. I learned so much about compassion and understanding from listening to your stories – many thanks.

Finally, this work would not be possible to get out to you, the reader, without the hard work done by Jamie Stangroom,

Jan Raeder – Self-Care Sensei

Paul Hendricks, Stephanie Blake, Diane Matthews, and George Oliver. You all made this vision a reality, and for that, I will be forever grateful.

# About the Author

With a master's degree in well-being education, Jan Raeder – The Self-Care Sensei has gained a deep understanding of the factors contributing to overall well-being. She has developed a holistic approach to helping others live well through her academic studies, encompassing techniques that develop mental resilience and emotional balance. Jan believes true well-being is achieved when all these aspects are nurtured and aligned.

# Foreword

Many folks hope to improve their health and well-being *and* are looking for a road map to get there. Unfortunately, many fail or get detoured on their journey.

Why are we looking for ways to be happier or more fulfilled? Sometimes, it happens when we reach a crossroads or a turning point. These can be big or small events, often different for everyone. In my experience, health-related crises, job loss, relationship ending, and age can be triggers. Do any of these resonate with you?

Over the last few years, there has been a collective watershed moment – **COVID-19**. The pandemic has made many of us question many things. My grandmother once told me, "That which does not kill us makes us stronger." This was originally said by the German philosopher Friedrich Nietzsche, and since hearing it for the first time, it has had a profound effect on the way I look at life's struggles. When faced with challenges, we can fight them and grow.

*"Out of suffering have emerged the strongest souls; the most massive characters are seared with scars."*

*– Khalil Gibran*

# Table of Contents

**INTRODUCTION** ..................................................... 1

**What exactly *is* wellness?** ........................................ 4

**Let's briefly breakdown those pillars…** ................... 11

    Meaning ................................................................. 12

    Optimism (Positive Emotions) ............................. 13

    Relationships ....................................................... 14

    Engagement ......................................................... 16

**The Flourishing Scale** ............................................. 23

    Scale ..................................................................... 24

    Flourishing Scale Statements ............................. 24

**MEANING** ................................................................. 26

**OPTIMISM & POSITIVE EMOTIONS** ..................... 44

**RELATIONSHIPS** ................................................... 66

**ENGAGEMENT** ....................................................... 91

**LET'S WRAP IT ALL UP** ........................................ 99

**APPENDIX** ..............................................................................116

**WORKS CITED** ...................................................................118

Strive for M.O.R.E

# INTRODUCTION

Hello! My name is Jan Raeder – the Self-Care Sensei – and I'm honored to have the opportunity to share some insights about well-being and wellness with you. For several years now, I've been working closely with people to enhance their personal well-being. Many of us want to make changes as we come out of an altered reality since early 2020. Many folks hope to improve their health and well-being *and* are looking for a road map to get there.

Psychologists use a term to describe the state that many folks are currently in – languishing[1]. It's the place between depression and flourishing. (More on the term flourishing as we move along!) You may be languishing right now, so you decided to get better acquainted with what researchers have been studying to help us feel more alive.

---

[1] "Languishing: the condition of absence of mental health, characterized by ennui, apathy, listlessness, and loss of interest in life" (American Psychological Association, 2023).

*(stock image)*

As far as the psychological community is concerned, this state is not a mental health problem. It's more of a lack of mental wellness. Sometimes, when we can find ways to put what we're experiencing into words, it can be easier to uncover ways to change our situation. And that's what we will try to do here in this book – uncover ways to change your situation. Over the coming pages, I want you to engage in true self-care by using the educational process[2] we'll cover to learn and grow.

With this guide to some of the science and some exercises that really work, enhancing and fine-tuning your well-being won't be so daunting. I hope to deconstruct or unravel the *abstract* realm of wellness/well-being for you!

---

[2] "Education is the only key to success in personal and professional life. Education provides us various types of knowledge and skills. It is a continuous, slow and secure process of learning which helps us in obtaining knowledge. It is a continuous process which starts when we take birth and ends when our life ends." (Srivastava, 2016).

Here is some more background for you. There are many expressions associated with quality of life. Words like - wellness, wellbeing, eudemonia, vigor, wholeness, and flourishing are all terms that can suggest personal satisfaction and health. Whatever word is used, **well-being** is both subjective and conceptual. The term **wellness** brings to mind the physical aspects of health – one's nutritional regime, exercise choices, and the like.

On the other hand, the word **well-being** is more closely associated with the spiritual and psychological aspects of living. This book will attempt to break down wellness **and** well-being. I want to empower you with a condensed understanding of some of the rich landscape of research that has been done regarding these concepts ***AND*** give you some evidence-based exercises you can start incorporating daily. While what I share with you here may sound very much like common sense, there is, in fact, solid scientific research behind living well, appreciating, and acknowledging that you are living a fulfilling life. We will be taking a dive into some of the scientific research here!

**Sound good? Great! Let's get started.**

# What exactly *is* wellness?

First, let's begin with an academic definition of wellness. The National Wellness Institute defines ***wellness*** as follows:

**"Wellness is an active process through which people become aware of, and make choices toward, a more successful existence."**

So, the quality of your life, and mine, is an <u>***ACTIVE***</u> process <u>**full**</u> of choices!

Research also provides a more systematic understanding of wellness by breaking it down into **8** Dimensions:

1) Emotional
2) Physical
3) Occupational
4) Social
5) Spiritual
6) Intellectual
7) Environmental
8) Financial[3]

---

[3] Image: (8 Dimensions of Well-being, https://www.csupueblo.edu/health-education-and-prevention/8-dimension-of-well-being.html)

There is a complex relationship between the mind (our brains) and the body regarding wellness and well-being. Since our brains are central to our daily functioning, we should take some time to jump in.

*"The human brain has 100 billion neurons, each neuron connected to 10 thousand other neurons. Sitting on your shoulders is the most complicated object in the known universe."*

*- Michio Kaku*

Dr. Kaku makes a bold observation about our miraculous brains. The human brain is definitely *the* most complicated part of the human anatomy. Neuroscientists and cognitive psychologists research our brains by looking at how they work, think, learn, remember events, and the like. Let's try to understand our

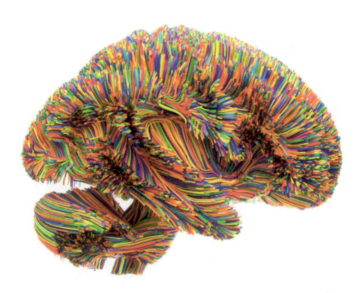

*(Stock Image)*

amazing brain and how it has changed throughout human history, shall we? Don't worry, it will be interesting, and most importantly, I will be brief! We are a very complicated species that has been through numerous revisions, if you will, over the last several million years. The Smithsonian Institution shares, "Human evolution is the lengthy process of change by which people originated from apelike ancestors. Scientific evidence shows that the physical and behavioral traits shared by all people originated from apelike ancestors and evolved over a period of approximately six million years" (2022).

In a wonderful TedTalk given by Dr. Daniel Gilbert, a social psychologist, author, and researcher, he shared some insights into how our brains have changed over time. Dr. Gilbert stated that much of our brain development only occurred in the past 2 million years. Specifically, the human brain gained almost two pounds and more structures (Gilbert, 2004). So, what does that bit of information about our brains mean to us today, and how do we consider well-being?

Well, Dr. Gilbert suggested that the development of the human brain, specifically the prefrontal cortex (the front part of our brain), has allowed us to "experience things in our heads before we try them out in real life" (Gilbert, 2004). So, right now, as you read this, you might be experiencing the tasks you have to complete today before your next work week or day starts, where you might go on a dream vacation, or dinner with family and friends may be playing out in your head right now before it happens. **OR** you might be thinking, "When is she going to wrap this up?" Well, I'm sorry, all of those plans for later will have to wait a little longer. We're just getting started!

What Dr. Gilbert also discovered about our brains during his research is that our prefrontal cortex often can get it wrong!

What?! Yes, sadly, it can! We've all experienced this. Let me give you some examples. Maybe you believed getting that promotion at work or sitting behind the wheel of a new car would be one of the happiest times of your life. Truthfully, for a time, it may have made your happy meter go off the charts, but alas, that new job ultimately tends to bring on more pressure and stress, and you might also discover the insurance rates for that new car are so much higher than for your old one! So, let's keep those thoughts about what's happening later to a minimum... okay?

So why is it important to have a basic understanding of how our brain works? (**By the way, more basic brain information will be covered later in this book.) Well, remember earlier when I mentioned the definition of wellness? The Wellness Institute included that wellness is about "making choices." Since we use the potentially faulty prefrontal cortex when making decisions most of the time, trying new things can be scary for some. The signals in the brain work in a sort of top-down system and can depend on our past experiences.

Consequently, we may have subconscious biases and aversions to something new. Additionally, our brains are lazy, according to Nobel laureate Daniel Kahneman. Much of our decision-making can be influenced by the "fast thinking" or the instinctive part of our brain (Kahneman, 2011). Why is this important when making choices? Most of the time, making a choice can mean making a *change*. And we as humans, for the most part, **hate** change! We love to continue doing what we know and are comfortable with. According to Kahneman, we love to function on a sort of autopilot or our "System 1", the fast-thinking, emotional, and instinctual portion of our brain. This "fast thinking" and the prefrontal cortex can play a role in how we influence our future lives.[4]

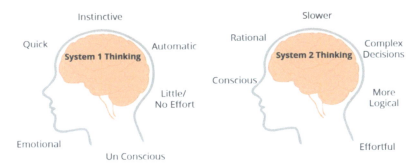

Wait, what... my choices for my future may be faulty because of the front of my brain?! How you choose to use your prefrontal cortex drives the answer to questions related to our well-being and living well. And this brings us back to what we call our comfort zones. We know that our comfort zone is the space we occupy that we feel most comfortable in, a place we know where our lazy brain (System 1) can operate on autopilot. Some of us look to the future or at something new and different with apprehension, sometimes even fear. The movie ticket you bought for the feature film playing on your prefrontal cortex may have been for a horror movie instead of an action/adventure. How do you play a different movie in your mind? How do you push beyond these comfort zones and go for changes, and better yet, why should you? The answer to this question is two-fold. It can be found in understanding what underpins our happiness or

---

[4] Image; (Catalyst)

the scaffolding of well-being and developing grit (more on *grit* as we move along). Research has shown that certain aspects of our lives directly relate to our wellbeing and more importantly these areas can and have been studied rigorously. Dr. Martin Seligman – one of the pioneers of the Positive Psychology[5] movement – has shown that human flourishing rests on certain areas of life (Seligman M., 2013). Those pillars include **m**eaning, **o**ptimism (or positive emotions), **r**elationships, and **e**ngagement. I like to think of this scaffolding using the acronym **M.O.R.E.** – to live well (or at least believe you are living a good life!), strive for **MORE**! It's an easy way to remember the areas that underpin wellbeing.

I would like to give you some background on Seligman's theory, which relates directly to ***well-being***. Wellbeing, happiness, or flourishing are all constructs that were/are in dire need of quantifiability. Seligman wished to test concepts and models that profess to make us happier or more fulfilled with scientific rigor[6]. Not only did he set out to understand ***what*** makes us happier, but he also endeavored to develop ways individuals and societies could raise their well-being levels. Pleasurable and unpleasurable states of consciousness or ***Hedonics***[7] are extremely subjective and, for the most part, unquantifiable. For example, if I ask you now if you are happy, depending on what happened

---

[5] "Positive psychology is the scientific study of what makes life worth living" (Peterson, 2014).

[6] Scientific rigor is the strict application of the scientific method to ensure unbiased and well-controlled experimental design, methodology, analysis, interpretation and reporting of results. www.nih.gov

[7] a branch of psychology that deals with pleasant and unpleasant states of consciousness and their relation to organic life.

before you started reading this passage the answer may be a resounding "YES!" Suppose I ask that same question again later in this book, and you have received a bad text from a friend or someone keeps interrupting you while trying to absorb this information. Your response may be, "No, I'm not happy at all!" Seligman's work proposes areas or pillars of well-being that can be measured subjectively and objectively. This framework and its components build upon one another and overlap. Seligman asserts that some of the pillars can be measured with rigor:

- **Meaning**
- **Optimism or Positive Emotion**
- **Engagement**

He also suggests that there are opportunities for improvement because of the ability to measure one's capacity with each of these aspects of well-being. Now, we are starting to get a glimpse of the road map to a life well lived!

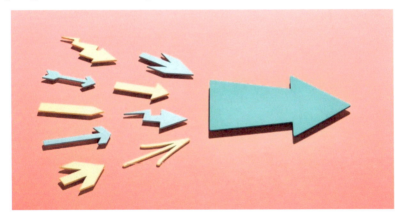

*(stock image)*

## Let's briefly breakdown those pillars…

*(stock image)*

## Meaning

*(stock image)*

Meaning is a very abstract construct. Seligman's work addresses personal meaning. Meaning relates to something bigger than yourself. Your spirituality, your faith, and your belief in a higher power are all facets of meaning. Okinawa, one of the *Blue Zones,* is an area of the world where a significant percentage of people live to be 100 years old. Research uncovered that the Okinawan centenarians who live long and healthy lives have what is referred to as "Ikigai" (Buettner, 2012). Simply put, Ikigai is why one gets out of bed in the morning. What is the purpose or meaning of your life?

## Optimism (Positive Emotions)

*(stock image)*

What is optimism? What are positive emotions? When you think of optimism, the first thing that might come to mind is, "The glass is always half full." At first blush, the term positive emotions may only suggest joy and happiness to you. However, optimism and positive emotions occupy many more domains. Interest, gratitude, inspiration, awe, hope, pride, amusement, and serenity are also additional positive emotions. Optimism suggests a choice or practice of erring on the side of positivity and hope. Research reveals that both positive emotions and optimism influence psychological states as well as cognition and enable us to see the bigger picture. Positive emotional states open individuals to change the confines of their thought processes and allow for a shift in outlook. Developing optimism and positive emotions allows us to become more creative, both intellectually and artistically. Positivity also bolsters our thirst for new information and experiences ***and*** lets us expand the self.

## Relationships

*(stock image)*

These can be personal, occupational, environmental, and the one I believe is of vital importance – the relationship you have with yourself. Why did ***relationships*** make the short list of wellbeing pillars? Because of the research outcomes from a very long longitudinal study[8], *The Grant Study*[9] – it's an ongoing study that began in 1938, more than 80 years ago! One of the most significant revelations that researchers observed over the

---

[8] In a longitudinal study, researchers repeatedly examine the same individuals to detect any changes that might occur over a period of time. Longitudinal studies are a type of correlational research in which researchers observe and collect data on a number of variables without trying to influence those variables.

[9] https://www.adultdevelopmentstudy.org/grantandglueckstudy

course of this 80+ year study was the single most important aspect of the human experience, which significantly contributes to our well-being: how we relate to one another. But what do these relationships essential to wellbeing look like? Well, scholars suggest that to have meaningful relationships that enhance well-being we should develop our listening skills, embrace diversity, trust more, be able to give and take criticism, and foster empathy and compassion. These elements all help to improve our relationship building.

## Engagement

*(stock image)*

In wellbeing, engagement is tied to positive emotions and leads one to lose oneself in an activity or to achieve flow. Academics define flow as intense and focused concentration on the here and now or being present in the moment, mindful (Csikszentmihalyi, 1996). As an example, when you are reading a book that can help you understand wellbeing more deeply (Ha!). Being in flow allows us to experience positive emotions such as inspiration, awe, and interest. How can we be more engaged? We can limit our screen time, spend more time in nature, and allow and plan for more me time. Education and engagement go hand in hand. We can all learn new strategies that will facilitate personal growth. This could be by engaging in activities that are problem-based. Challenging ourselves and engaging in activities that push us beyond where we are now is difficult and takes courage. Find something you love and work hard at it. Failure will happen, but fulfillment and mastery will follow. We can explore what we already know, but when we go outside our comfort zones, we discover new areas in which we can develop and grow.

*(stock image)*

*"The credit belongs to the man who is actually in the arena, whose face is marred by dust and sweat and blood; who strives valiantly; who errs, who comes short again and again, because there is no effort without error and shortcoming; but who does actually strive to do the deeds; who knows the great enthusiasms, the great devotions; who spends himself in a worthy cause; who at best knows, in the end, the triumph of high achievement, and who at the worst, if he fails, at least fails while daring greatly, so that his place shall never be with those cold and timid souls who neither know victory nor defeat."*

*– Theodore Roosevelt*

In the next chapters of this book, we will be drilling down further into the pillars. We'll also learn some interventions, or what I am going to refer to as "Wellbeing Wazas [10]" (techniques), you can use to improve the areas which support our subjective wellbeing. Additional references for further study – if you so desire – are included in an appendix at the end of this book. Additionally, throughout this text, you will come across sections where you will see this graphic:

This is the Self-Care Sensei logo, and I'm using it here in this book to interject information that may be somewhat off-topic but, in some cases, still relevant or just plain fun to learn!

---

[10] Waza means technique in karate!

I call these areas "Invigorate Your Intellect." I truly believe lasting self-care is based on the educational process. (Hint, hint *** practicing **engagement**!) When we take the time to learn new things and apply them, we are taking care of ourselves on a higher, long-lasting level.

But first, I should share a bit about myself to allow you to connect with my story and why helping people understand the science of wellbeing is so important to me.

We've all heard that our story is unique. While I agree with this to a certain extent, I do believe there is a lot of overlap in the human experience. I believe we all suffer, we all experience joy, we all eventually have some health issue, and we all have something to offer. I guess finding our own voice is what separates us from others. My voice is one of crying out for people to act AND take responsibility for their own wellbeing! Happiness, joy, and life satisfaction come from within; the good news is that you can learn how to be happier.

So, who am I anyway? Well, I have always been of service to others, whether that was in the healthcare field or instructing people in the physical fitness industry. The bulk of my personal history comes from studying Okinawan/Japanese martial arts: karate.

When I took my first karate class, I was hooked. That was more than thirty years ago! My personal journey in martial arts has been filled with overcoming challenges, inner exploration, understanding, and embracing Bushidō (Warrior Spirit).

Warrior spirit, fearlessness, duty, and honor are words that can be used to describe what a lifelong student of karate embraces; these terms represent who I am.

Throughout my many years of martial arts education, I have learned about culture, history, self-awareness, self-defense, psychology, leadership, perseverance, nutrition, meditation, self-discipline, and compassion, to name a few. Over those many years of teaching karate, kickboxing, yoga, and meditation, I have had the privilege to be an instrument of change in many people's lives. Some of my students would tell you that I love quotes, clichés, and sayings – and that would be true! I think they help us to understand and remember things more readily. I know both my grandmothers used them all the time as I was growing up! Clichés somehow seem to simplify complicated things.

There is something to be said for pushing yourself past what you believe are your limits. I believe the self-discipline and Bushidō I gained from karate training prepared me for my return to higher education. It equipped me with the tenacity I needed to accomplish my goals. One of my goals was to earn both a bachelor's *and* master's degree within four years. Employing self-discipline and perseverance allowed me to accomplish that lofty goal! In 2013, I re-entered college after a thirty-year detour of sorts. I only had nineteen credits from my first try at higher education in

the early 1980s. I graduated in 2015 with a Bachelor of Science before deciding to get right back to work in the fall of 2015. I then enrolled in a master's program and completed my studies in the winter of 2017.

Pursuing goals is not done in a vacuum. I'm sure you can relate to that. We set goals, and then life shows up, sometimes with a vengeance! I, like many of you, have not escaped life's vengeance. As I mentioned earlier about the human experience overlap, I, too, have suffered from it. I've battled with depression and anxiety, been diagnosed with health issues, experienced tragedies, and had my share of dealing with difficult people (family, friends, and colleagues). Despite all that, I try to live my life in the present. The tenets of meditation teach us that the past and the future do not exist. These states, past and future, are a source of suffering for many (we'll address this further as we go along). However, due to my daily practice of bringing myself back to the present moment, I have let go of much of what happened in my past. One thing is for certain, though: I have chosen to use my past as a tool to shape both my current state of contentment and hopefulness. You can learn to do this, too, with regular practice! YAY!

*(stock image)*

## The Flourishing Scale

\*\*Before we begin to really dig deep into these pillars and Wellbeing Wazas, let's get a starting point for how well you perceive your life to be at this point in time. This is just a way to measure your baseline before you start applying the knowledge you gain from this book. Please record this somewhere so you can refer to it later. ***Thanks!***

This is a brief **8**-item assessment used to measure the respondent's self-perceived success in important areas such as relationships, self-esteem, purpose, and optimism. The Flourishing Scale provides a psychological well-being score (Diener et al., 2009).

Below is Diener's *Flourishing Scale*, consisting of **8** statements with which you may agree or disagree. Using the **1–7** scale below, indicate your level of agreement with each statement.

**Scale**

1 - Strongly disagree

2 - Disagree

3 - Slightly disagree

4 - Mixed or neither agree nor disagree

5 - Slightly agree

6 - Agree

7 - Strongly agree

**Flourishing Scale Statements**

1 - I lead a purposeful and meaningful life

2 - My social relationships are supportive and rewarding

3 - I am engaged and interested in my daily activities

4 - I actively contribute to the happiness and well-being of others

5 - I am competent and capable in the activities that are important to me

6 - I am a good person and live a good life

7 - I am optimistic about my future

8 - People respect me

Scoring: Add the responses from **1** to **7** for all eight items. The lowest possible score is **8,** while the highest is **56**. When

Diener used this test for some university students, 573 of them, they had an average score of 45.4 (Diener, 2009).

\*\*\*A high score represents a person with many psychological resources and strengths.

Well, how did you do? When I originally took this test at the start of my return to college, my score wasn't good at all. During my first semester, I took a class that was geared toward understanding personal wellness. My score was 24. Yup, **24**! However, over the past several years, I've been doing the Well-being Wazas (that we'll be covering here) daily, and today my score is 52!

While that's a great score, I do believe (for me anyway) there's always room for improvement. Additionally, it's very easy to drop back into old habits that seem to be burned into our memories and buried deep in System 1. With this endeavor, like many others – e.g., fitness, psychological work, and learning goals – persistent work is required. Sorry to tell you this, folks, self-improvement is never complete!

When I mentioned earlier that I try not to live in the past, one important thing I did learn from my past is that we are all stronger than we realize. So, let's roll up our sleeves and get deeper into those pillars!

*(stock image)*

# MEANING

*(stock image)*

***"There are only two ways to live your life. One is as though nothing is a miracle. Another is as though everything is a miracle." – Albert Einstein.***

As I may have mentioned earlier, I love quotes and clichés. I am especially fond of Albert Einstein's quotes, and this is one of my favorites. I truly believe it goes right to the heart of both wellness and well-being (remember our definition - ***Wellness is an active process***) as well as the very abstract concept of MEANING. The reason Einstein hit the nail on the head with this quote is that it's ***your*** choice; you can take the optimistic view (erring on the side of positivity), or you can choose a flat, listless, pessimistic view of life. When you choose a positive "everything is a miracle" view, you are generally grasping meaning in your life. So why do scholars include "meaning" as one of the foundational pieces of well-being, and what does that actually *mean*? Hmmmm…well, let's try to make some sense of it.

There has been much research done regarding the connection between religion/spirituality and wellness. Scholars have consistently shown that those who are religious/spiritual are happier and more satisfied with life. What does it mean to be religious/spiritual? One scholar who did a meta-analysis[11] of the research on religion/spirituality, health, and wellness shared a comprehensive definition of spirituality that I want to share with you here:

"Spirituality is distinguished from all other things—humanism, values, morals, and mental health—by its connection to that which is sacred, the transcendent. The transcendent is that which is outside of the self, and yet also within the self—and in Western traditions, is called God, Allah, HaShem, or a Higher Power, and in Eastern traditions may be called Brahman, manifestations of Brahman, Buddha, Dao, or ultimate truth/reality. Spirituality is intimately connected to the supernatural, the mystical, and organized religion, although it also extends beyond organized religion (and begins before it). Spirituality includes both a search for the transcendent and the discovery of the transcendent and so involves traveling along the path that leads from nonconsideration to questioning to either staunch nonbelief or belief and, if belief, then ultimately to devotion and finally, surrender. Thus, our definition of spirituality is very similar to religion, and there is clearly overlap" (Koenig, 2012).

---

[11] *Meta-analysis* is a statistical process that combines the data of multiple studies to find common results and to identify overall trends.

12

There were several elements of this definition that spoke to me, but the last part really jumped out: "Spirituality is very similar to religion, and there is clearly overlap." This shows that when researchers have access to human participants, the answers to the study questions rarely turn out to be black and white. I guess that is why trying to understand what works to make us happier can be so abstract!

In a recent Gallup article, the author stated, "Weekly religious service attenders are, in fact, more likely to say they are very satisfied than are those who make $100,000 or more in annual household income" (Newport PhD, 2022). Now, that is a

---

[12] Image; (ThePirateKing777)

very powerful statement! This is what excites me so much about digging into research! When you take the time to read the studies for yourself, there is so much to learn. Let's now get back to what some of the research about religious affiliations has revealed. Depending on age and experiences growing up, it would appear that people have varying views on religious affiliation. Researchers found that participants who were raised in a household that participated in formal religion were more likely to get involved in their communities and feel less lonely (Cox, 2022).

On the other hand, those whose upbringing was devoid of religious traditions had quite different views. This is not to say that religious and/or non-religious affiliated folks don't volunteer in their communities and feel more connected. Interestingly, this same study revealed there was more of a propensity for those who were both educated *and* religious to be more civic-minded (Cox, 2022).

You may be thinking, "I don't participate in any formal religion." You are not alone. Researchers found that study participants separated from their religious institutions for various reasons. When first thinking about this issue, the pandemic and scandals came to my mind. Diving in, the author shared, "Evidence paints a much more complicated picture than the traditional narrative" (Cox, 2022).

I know some of you reading this may have never read a research study. Lots of us get our information through someone else's lens. I will admit we are doing that here to a degree. However, I really encourage you to read at least one study for yourself. Below, I offer a bit of insight into research.

## *Invigorate Your Intellect*

*Some of you reading this may be familiar with research, and some may not. I'm not going to get into a whole lesson on all the different methodologies out there. Still, if you wish to dive into this deeper, I have included in the appendix a few resources to help. The types of methodologies that are regularly used in psychological research are quantitative[13], qualitative[14], and mixed*

---

[13] Quantitative research is the process of collecting and analyzing numerical data. It can be used to find patterns and averages, make predictions, test causal relationships, and generalize results to wider populations. (Pathak, Jena, & Kalra, 2013)

[14] Qualitative research involves collecting and analyzing non-numerical data (e.g., text, video, or audio) to understand concepts, opinions, or experiences. It can be used to gather in-depth insights into a problem or generate new ideas for research. (Bhandari, 2020)

*methods. Why is it important to briefly understand research methodology? Well, some areas of science depend on diverse types of research. There has always been a debate between "hard" and "soft" sciences. Examples of hard sciences include physics, biology, and chemistry. Whereas soft sciences are centered more on sociology, psychology and the like and have more to do with behavior, thoughts, and feelings. These particular aspects of soft sciences make for a more complicated approach when trying to answer research questions. In regard to soft sciences, it's important to take note that research results can be harder to replicate (particularly important when testing with rigor). Because there are people involved (the study participants), there can be variables that change from study group to study group when a different researcher tries to replicate a study. Therefore, I have dedicated myself to helping people understand what interventions (Wellbeing Wazas – what I call them here in this book) have been tested with rigor and what seems to really "work" in moving toward a life well lived.*

---

Let's get back to unpacking **MEANING**…

Whatever our opinions and experiences with religious beliefs, affiliations, and the like might be, the findings of multiple studies over decades are why researchers have made meaning (spirituality/religious beliefs) an underpinning of *subjective wellbeing*.[15] The correlation between religious beliefs and wellbeing, time and time again, has shown that those who are religious/spiritual believe there is something much larger in life than themselves and have a greater degree of wellbeing (Koenig, 2012). I don't want this to go off on a tangent of religion vs non-religion. The research is clear: supporting and bolstering meaning in our lives equals greater wellness.

While meaning is definitively tied to our belief in something beyond ourselves, it is also part of our day-to-day experiences. What do I *mean* by that? Well, for millennia, humans have been looking for understanding. Not only have we been trying to understand what is all around us, but also what is within us. The overarching questions for many are, "Why am I here?" and "What is my purpose?" It's important for me to say that I'm not sure if there are concrete answers to both of those questions. I'm also not here (nor is this book) proposing to answer them. What we are trying to do here is gain a better understanding of what research has to offer and what some daily activities (Wellbeing Wazas) can help to move us in the direction of our "best lives."

In addition to our spirituality, knowing what holds meaning in our lives is important. This is where things get a bit tricky and even more abstract. Every person has a different view of what is important to them.

While there is overlap, e.g., love, family, friends, health, freedom, etc. – these aspects of life can look different for each

---

[15] "a person's cognitive and affective evaluations of his or her life. Simply, SWB (subjective wellbeing) is the individual evaluation of quality of life." - Ed Deiner

one of us. And with that, it's time for our first "Wellbeing Waza!"

I should first explain what a "Waza" is. I thought it would be fun to interject some of my karate background into this eBook. I decided to call the interventions (daily activities) "Wellbeing Wazas." A Waza in karate is a technique. Practicing "techniques" allows for improvement. When you engage in the daily practice of the Wellbeing Wazas in this book, you will be able to improve your wellbeing.

Additionally, I will also be throwing around the word "Ren ma." Ren ma in Karate-Do[16] means constant improvement or polishing. I have found in many aspects of life where change is involved, consistency (and *grit*!) is key. This is why the self-discipline that is learned in the study of karate, athletics, and academics – many things really – is so important to building a better life. We will go over this more in later sections of the book! But for now, back to your Wellbeing Waza!

---

[16] Karate means "empty hand" and Do means "the way."

## "WHAT DO YOU VALUE MOST?"

On the next page is a chart with over one hundred values. Give yourself about fifteen to twenty minutes to look them over and choose ten that best represent you. After choosing the ten, narrow it down further by creating a list of your top five. These top five must be in order of importance to you! This may sound simple, but I assure you that it is not. Once you've done it, you'll begin to have some more insight into yourself and the meaning of your own life.

Take your time with this exercise. I'll see you on the other side!

## Strive for M.O.R.E

| Achievement | Acknowledge-ment | Adventure | Authenticity | Beauty |
|---|---|---|---|---|
| Challenge | Change | Cleanness | Collaboration | Commitment |
| Common Sense | Communication | Community | Competence | Compassion |
| Connection | Cooperation | Courage | Creativity | Decisiveness |
| Design | Democracy | Discipline | Discovery | Diversity |
| Ease | Efficiency | Equality | Excellence | Exceptionalism |
| Expertise | Fairness | Faith | Faithfulness | Family |
| Freedom | Friendship | Fun | Genius | Globalism |
| Goodwill | Goodness | Gratitude | Hard Work | Harmony |
| Health | Honesty | Honor | Humanity | Independence |
| Individuality | Inner Peace | Innovation | Integrity | Intimacy |
| Ingenuity | Joy | Justice | Knowledge | Law |
| Leadership | Love | Loyalty | Meaning | Merit |
| Money | Openness | Order | Originality | Patriotism |

| | | | | |
|---|---|---|---|---|
| Peace | Perfection | Personal Growth | Pleasure | Power |
| Practicality | Preservation | Privacy | Progress | Prosperity |
| Purity | Quality | Regularity | Reliability | Resourcefulness |
| Respect | Responsiveness | Safety | Security | Self-love |
| Service | Sexuality | Simplicity | Skillfulness | Spirituality |
| Stability | Status | Strength | Success | Teamwork |
| Tolerance | Tradition | Trust | Truth | Unity |
| Vitality | Will | Wellbeing | Wisdom | Youthfulness |

***Congratulations!*** Well, how did you do? Did any of your choices surprise you?

My top five are Gratitude, Compassion, Beauty, Service, and Discipline. I have to admit that I found this exercise to be very difficult. There were so many values that I identify with and are important to me. Despite that, I can safely say these top five definitely represent me. I am grateful for everything and everyone in my life, as well as being grateful for life itself. Compassion, I believe, is so important for a well-lived life. Not only having compassion for myself but also for *all* people (and sentient beings) I encounter. When I say "encounter," that also means people I see on television, social media, in public service, and the like. We have all heard the saying, "Walk a mile in my shoes." So, here we go again with an Invigorate Your Intellect moment!

## *Invigorate Your Intellect*

*The original quote was, "Take the time to walk a mile in his moccasins." ~ Mary T. Lathrap, 1895*

*Mary T. Lathrap was a 19$^{th}$-century American author, poet, and suffragist. In 1895, she penned a poem titled "Judge Softly." The poem speaks to how we should treat one another while being an ode to compassion and empathy. In case you are interested, there are links in the references to the poem (shared by James Milson) as well as some more information about Mary. As always, if you are interested!*

---

Now, let's go back to my top five. When I think of beauty and why it's third on my list, it doesn't actually have to do with an individual's physical beauty. Beauty in this context has to do with appreciating the beauty of nature around us, appreciation for beautiful sounds we hear, respect for incredible skills folks have and the like. Service is number four for me, as I have always been of service to others. I'm a giver. It brings me so much joy to help others and be a part of their "a-ha!" moments. Discipline rounds out my top five because I have learned throughout my life that discipline, specifically self-discipline, is critical to a happy life. Most folks don't want to answer to anyone, and I believe that is not realistic. To have a truly happy life, being kind, of service, and generous to others is important. Many of us feel great when we can do something for others, and there are loads of scientific studies to back that up – but I'm sure you have heard that before! I'm now going to circle back to the first value on my list: gratitude.

While it has become sort of a buzzword lately, gratitude is a positive emotion with transcendent qualities. What does that mean, "transcendent qualities?" Remember our definition of spirituality earlier in this section? "The transcendent is that which is outside of the self, and yet also within the self."

When we are grateful, more importantly when we practice gratitude regularly (daily really), we connect to the divine, a higher power, etc.

*(stock image)*

We can lift our mood immediately by practicing gratitude. I know many of you may have heard about keeping a gratitude journal, and I'm not here to disagree with gratitude journals or lists; some have great success with them. We are here to learn what has been proven to enhance our wellbeing. Science shows that for some, keeping a gratitude journal or list can become tedious or rote (Regan, Walsh, & Lyubomirsky, 2022). If you are the type of person who has started to journal repeatedly only to lose interest, maybe that's not the right activity for you. I will confess I have tried journaling, and it never seems to work out for me. I have multiple ***empty,*** pretty journals to prove it! Here's where we come to another Wellbeing Waza.

*This Wellbeing Waza is called:*

## "WHAT WENT WELL"

This exercise was first developed by Dr. Martin Seligman and his psychology students. Dr. Seligman is a self-proclaimed pessimist. We really aren't taught to think positively; in fact, we are hard-wired for negativity – more on that in the next section of this book. This exercise helps to shift our thinking and ground us in what is meaningful in our lives. It's simple, really: each day, try and consider three or more (or it could even be less) *things* that went well during your day. They don't have to be big things; they can be small things. Once you have determined the events that went well, the next part of the exercise is actually the most important. **Why** did those things go well? This is very different than writing things in a gratitude journal. To shift our thinking, we need to take the extra step to consider *why* these things went well. If you want to take the time to write these daily events down, feel free. This is the exercise I do right before I go to bed. It's part of my nighttime ritual. I truly believe that it has improved my sleep, reminded me of what is meaningful for me on a daily basis, and also set me up for a positive day. I don't generally write down my "What Went Well" events, as journaling for me is a bit tedious and awkward, as mentioned earlier.

For parents who are reading this, this is a fantastic exercise to do with your children. If you are a family that makes the time to have a meal together, this is a great time to share; if you are too busy for a family sit-down meal, make this part of your kids' bedtime routine. Kids can learn from your example and begin to look for what is positive and meaningful for them throughout their day. This can also serve as a wonderful opportunity to stay connected with your kids!

For those who work with others, whether you are part of a team or a team leader, this is also a wonderful exercise to include during meetings and the like. It not only keeps the positivity flowing but brings teams together by circling back to what is meaningful while also providing an avenue for all to feel like they are being heard and included.

Seligman's research showed that those who suffered from depression and utilized this exercise saw a marked improvement in their mood (Seligman, 2012, Seligman; Flourish: Positive Psychology, 2010). There have been other researchers who have undertaken studies using What Went Well (or Three Good Things) as an intervention. In a more recent study, research subjects were neonatal healthcare workers, e.g., nurses and physicians with a high rate of burnout. Study participants were asked to use the What Went Well exercise online daily for fourteen days. While the full group of eighty-nine participants did not finish the study, thirty-two participants did. The results showed that the What Went Well exercise "creates a structure that allows participants to reflect on frequent but relatively simple and small doses of positive emotion" (Rippstein-Leuenberger, Mauthner, Sexton, & Schwendimann, 2017). As I mentioned earlier in this book, there is a lot of overlap with our **M.O.R.E** theory. Finding meaning in life is tied to cultivating positive emotions and optimism. Additionally, there are no negative side effects from this or any of the Wellbeing Wazas!

This is a great segue to our next section – Optimism & Positive Emotions. Let's dive in!

*(stock image)*

## OPTIMISM & POSITIVE EMOTIONS

*(stock image)*

*"It is during our darkest moments that we must focus to see the light."*

*- Aristotle*

Optimism and positive emotions are a choice, right? Research suggests that genetics does play a role in whether we are optimistic or pessimistic (Bates, 2015; Mosing et al., 2009). So, how much do our genes influence our happiness, then? There has been some scholarship that suggests up to fifty percent of our happiness depends on our genetics (Lyubomirsky S. S., 2005). And like any subject in academia or scientific circles, there are others who disagree (Kashdan, 2015). I believe it is important to note that these folks are talking about *happiness*. Think back to the beginning of this book; researchers who are trying to unravel, with rigor, what enhances our wellbeing don't necessarily like the term "happiness." Happiness can be fleeting and fluctuate very quickly depending on input and circumstances. Let's bring our focus back to wellbeing and add to our understanding of the argument as to why we shouldn't be grasping for the happiness "brass ring."

## *Invigorate Your Intellect*

"Grabbing the brass ring" or getting a "shot at the brass ring" also means striving for the highest prize or living life to the fullest. It's not clear when the phrase came into wide use, but it has been found in dictionaries as far back as the late 19th century.

A brass ring is a small grabbable ring that a dispenser presents to a carousel rider during the course of a ride. Usually, there are a large number of iron or steel rings and one brass ring. It takes some dexterity to grab a ring from the dispenser as the carousel rotates. The iron rings can be tossed at a target as an amusement. Typically, getting the brass ring gets the rider some sort of prize when presented to the operator. The prize is often a free repeat ride.

The figurative phrase to grab the brass ring is derived from this device.

*Brass ring devices were developed during the heyday of the carousel in the U.S.—about 1880 to 1921. At one time, the riders on the outside row of horses were often given a little challenge, perhaps as a way to draw interest or build excitement, more often as an enticement to sit on the outside row of horses, which frequently did not move up and down and were, therefore, less enticing by themselves. Most rings were iron, but one or two per ride were made of brass; if a rider managed to grab a brass ring, it could be redeemed for a free ride. References to a literal brass ring go back to the 1890s.*

*As the carousel began to turn, rings were fed to one end of a wooden arm that was suspended above the riders. Riders hoped that the timing of the carousel rotation (and the rise-and-fall motion of their seat when movable seats were included in the outer circle of the carousel) would place them within reach of the dispenser when a ring (and preferably a brass ring) was available (Brass ring, 2022).*

---

Let's continue to try and grab for the "brass ring" of flourishing! Remember what I mentioned earlier about our brains? They developed quickly over the last few million years, giving us a better opportunity for imagination. Our brains are also wired for negativity. You can say that negativity is part of our survival mechanisms. We needed it to survive when there were multiple physical threats. We needed to focus on those threats to avoid potentially harmful situations. We have developed what researchers call "negativity bias." Scholars suggest that we "attend to, learn from, and use negative information far more than positive information" (Vaish, 2008). WOW! No wonder we are bombarded with bad news, catastrophe reports, and other doom and gloom. (hint, hint…this ties into one of our upcoming Wellbeing Wazas!) It seems like the media has figured out that we can't help but have a voracious appetite for this kind of input.

Gallup conducts regular surveys to determine the emotional state of the world. Surveyors ask participants questions related to their experiences and record their responses. Unfortunately, according to Gallup, "While 2020 may have been a record-setting year for negative emotions, the world has been on a negative trajectory for almost a decade" (Ray, 2021). Gallup suggests that some of the increased negativity of late has been due to the pandemic. However, these elevated levels of stress, worry, sadness, and anger have been on the rise since 2006. Check your levels of stress/negativity right now by asking yourself about your experiences from yesterday:

How much sadness did you experience?

How much worry did you experience?

How much physical pain did you experience?

How much stress did you experience?

How much anger did you feel yesterday?

Take a few moments to reflect on these five questions. These are the same questions that Gallup uses when they survey people worldwide to determine Global Emotions. In my experience and academic work, these questions speak to perspective. I guess the reason you may have decided to understand wellbeing better is that you want to *change* your perspective. We all react to our current circumstances. Our reactions and perspectives are based on both genetic predispositions and life experiences. Remember what I said earlier when I was introducing myself? We **ALL** experience trauma, loss, sadness, tragedy, and the like. What is in our power is *how* we react and perceive these events.

Remember the question I asked at the beginning of this section – Optimism and positive emotions are a choice, right? Yes, they certainly can be!

> *"How hard is it to decide to be in a good mood and be in a good mood?"*
>
> *– John Cusack (Say Anything)*

I love this line from a movie you may or may not have seen; it was popular in the late 80s. John Cusack's character is speaking to his sister (played by Joan Cusack), who is a bit pessimistic in the film. True to the character, she replies (dripping with sarcasm!!), "Gee, it's *easy*."

I truly believe, based on my personal experience and the numerous studies I have read, that you can *choose* to be positive. The ability to carry out this choice or to be successful at choosing to be positive depends on how you plan on attacking this decision. You see, I think it is not just a choice; it's a practice. Remember earlier when I mentioned the term Ren ma? In karate circles, Ren ma means polishing. We must constantly practice and polish our practice over and over and over again. But how? Well, that's what we are working on here, YAY!

Here's another Wellbeing Waza!

*Wellbeing Waza for boosting positivity:*

## "STOP WATCHING THE NEWS!!!!"

Gathering data always helps when you are unsure if something is going to work for you. Choose when you are going to start your trial of "no news." Take the time to jot down how you are feeling at the beginning of your test run. Then, stop watching for at least ten days to two weeks. At the end of the trial, reflect on how you are feeling. ***Ta Da***!! You should be feeling a bit better, and this will encourage you to continue staying away from those news channels on your television, phone, tablet, computer, or wherever you have been getting your regular doses of added negativity!

Okay, some of you may be saying, "I can't do that! I need to know what is going on in the world." I don't want to get into a debate about media outlets whose reporting is accurate, yada yada yada… (Seinfeld reference, ha!). If we take a step back and drop political and personal views and look at the media as the business they are, ***every*** outlet has an agenda – to make money, keep their sponsorship, and KEEP YOU WATCHING (or reading)! We have already established that we suffer from negativity bias and gravitate toward negative input. News outlets know this and capitalize on it. I don't disagree that we should stay informed. However, watching the news cycle over and over is a recipe for negativity. Barbara Fredrickson, positive emotion researcher and scholar, shares, "surveys show that the more people watch television, the more violent they judge the world to be.

You might think that those who watch a lot of TV are simply better informed about the evils of the world. They're not. They grossly overestimate rates of violence. People who watch less TV are more accurate judges of the degree of risk we all might encounter each day" (Fredrickson B., 2009).

Personally, I watch very little to no news *at all*. The weather is something I keep up with as it contributes to my clothing choices and so on. Even the weather has been turned into a twenty-four-hour news cycle input for us! An additional reason for staying away from or, at the very least, greatly limiting your exposure to the news comes from understanding our stress response.

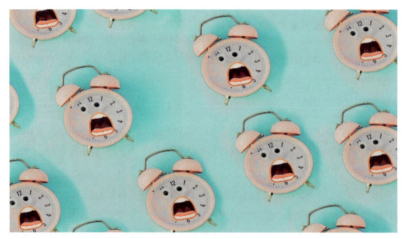

*(stock image)*

I'm only going to highlight some of the basics of the stress response. Some of you may be familiar with this, some not. Earlier, we talked about negativity bias and the survival part of why we have a propensity for negativity. What's interesting about our stress response is that it's the same whether we are being chased by a wild animal or if we are under pressure to complete a task at work. The big difference between the animal threat versus the project at-work *threat* is duration. When our ancestors went into the fight or flight mode to avoid being killed by a predator, their parasympathetic nervous system[17] kicked in just as soon as the threat had passed, thus bringing the body back into balance. Today, our stressors are ongoing. Let's take the twenty-four-hour news cycle I'm asking you to take a step away from. Tragic stories are reported daily and then repeated again and again and again. Consciously, we know that it's the same story that is being reported, but subconsciously, our stress response is ignited again and again and again. The same happens when work projects or personal stressors are present in our lives. We respond the same way physiologically as we would if we were being chased by an apex predator.

---

[17] "The parasympathetic part of your autonomic nervous system balances your sympathetic nervous system. While your sympathetic nervous system controls your body's "fight or flight" response, your parasympathetic nervous system helps to control your body's response during times of rest" (Cleveland Clinic, 2022).

# Strive for M.O.R.E

*(stock image)*

Think about this for a moment. When you watch the news and hear about tragedies, are you able to ***do*** anything about it anyway? In most cases, no.

Well, I don't know about you, but I think I've gone on enough about negativity! If you're anything like me – the consummate optimist – I can really start to feel the negative seeping in. Yuck! So, let's move on to why optimism and positivity are definitely a practice that you want to adopt.

Studying our emotions has been going on for decades. Many researchers have chosen to study negative emotions as they are easier to recognize and abundant. However, while all her colleagues were studying negative emotions, one scholar wanted to take the "road less traveled" and study positive emotions. We'll come back to her in a moment, but first, it's time to Invigorate Your Intellect again!

## *Invigorate Your Intellect*

### The Road Less Traveled

*This line comes from a poem titled, 'The Road Not Taken,' by the American poet Robert Frost (1874-1963). It originates from the English expression, 'to take the road less traveled,' which is often used as a means of celebrating individualism.*

*This, however, is a misinterpretation of the poem's meaning in its original context, which primarily deals with ideas of emotional unrest associated with decision-making.*

*I shall be telling this with a sigh*

*Somewhere ages and ages hence:*

**Two roads diverged in a wood, and I—**

**I took the one less traveled by**,

*And that has made all the difference.*

(The Road Not Taken, 16-20)

## Strive for M.O.R.E

*Frost wrote the poem in 1915, intended as a joke for his English friend, Edward Thomas. According to an exchange of letters between the two, the poem refers to frequent walks they would take through wooded paths while Frost lived in England for a time. When they came to forks in the trails, they'd choose one path. Afterward, Thomas would invariably lament not having taken the other, expressing that it could have been the more beautiful of the two.*

*In his letter, Frost wrote with friendly banter, "No matter which road you take, you'll always sigh and wish you'd taken another."*

*In the poem, the two paths are ultimately described as equally desirable options. In this sense, Frost explores and satirizes the notion of regret surrounding the unanswerable (and arguably unnecessary) question, "what if?" Because who can know with certainty whether one way will turn out better than the other? So why dwell in the what-ifs, and why not dwell in the beauty of the here and now?* (Roden)

*\*I love that Frost has determined that being in the present is beautiful!*

---

Barbara Fredrickson has been studying positive emotions for over thirty years. Her work has had a profound impact on the way I look at the world today. I have always been an optimist. However, as time moved on in my life with my exposure to various life and health events, my positive outlook shifted slightly. For a time, I didn't recognize myself. This turn of events was part of what fueled my academic endeavors and my need to understand why I was losing myself. After all, it's been said that "all research is 'me-search'." In Frederickson's book *Positivity*, she shares one story from two different perspectives. It's just a simple account of a family getting ready for their day. In one version (the *nothing* is a miracle version), the children interrupt their mom's attempt to start taking some *me-time* before rising. The kids lose shoes, chaos ensues, and tension builds, creating a bad day before it has even begun. Fredrickson shares the same scenario told from a positive perspective (the *everything* is a miracle version) where lost shoes become a game, and interruptions are an opportunity to share precious time with children who will be fully grown in no time at all. This positive perspective, *practice* as I have suggested here, spills over into the rest of the day, creating a solid, positive foundation for the parents to interact with colleagues during their workday. Think about that for just a moment.

*(stock image)*

Consider one of your recent days. Did you lose something – your keys, maybe? Or break or drop something – your cup of coffee? Or did your kids whine about something they wanted or interrupt you while you were trying to answer emails? Did your whole day seem to go down in flames before it even started? We've all had this happen. What is so impactful about bad things happening to us is that those events invade our thoughts and emotions. Negativity bias strikes again! This is where Fredrickson's work can have an impact on your daily life, too. Time for another Wellbeing Waza!

*For this Wellbeing Waza:*

## "STOP NEGATIVITY BIAS IN ITS TRACKS!"

When something goes wrong during your day, I want you to counterbalance it with at least **three** good things or thoughts. Try to do something that you really enjoy, or listen to some upbeat music or take the time to remember an event that you loved – preferably all three!! Additionally, change your thinking. Instead of focusing and latching on to the negative aspects of your day, reflect on the positive, very similar to the What Went Well exercise we discussed earlier. As a matter of fact, that exercise (if you are doing it daily) will help you counterbalance these bad things you and all of us experience daily. Fredrickson's work revealed that when bad things/thoughts happen, we need to offset them with at least three good things/thoughts, referred to as the 3 – to – 1 ratio (Fredrickson B., Are You Getting Enough Positivity in Your Diet? 2011). Since I am trying to make sure I keep this as balanced as I possibly can, I will mention that she did get some push back on this (Brown NJ, 2013). To clarify, the scholars who reviewed Fredrickson's work were troubled by her use of mathematical equations – the critics felt Frederickson and her team didn't nail the math. She did respond to their critique, saying that more research is needed and, "Science, at its best, self-corrects. We may now be witnessing such self-correction in action as mathematically precise statements about positivity ratios give way to heuristic[18] statements such as 'higher is better, within bounds'" (Pursuit of Happiness, 2023).

As I said earlier, in academic circles, there are always differing opinions and a need for more research. This kind of debate is good. This kind of feedback keeps the conversation moving forward! The downside is that it can get very confusing for the layperson.[19] To avoid some of this confusion, educate yourself – which is kind of what we are working on here. Take a look at the resources I've shared at the end of this book so that you, too, can read the studies for yourself.

Back to Fredrickson's ratio. In order to retrain your negativity-grabbing brain, you need to *practice* positivity. Fredrickson shares, "The multitude of studies that I and other scientists have conducted on positivity is destined to remain merely interesting dinner conversation until you deepen your self-study. You need to pivot away from what's worked for others and toward what works for you. Have your own "Eureka!" moments. Discover for yourself what rouses genuine and heartfelt positivity" (Fredrickson B., 2009). What does this positivity practice look like? Well, for one, consistency is key (practice ***grit***[20]). Change only comes from consistency, self-love, compassion, and self-discipline. Let me say that again –

---

[18] Heuristic: "A heuristic in psychology is a mental shortcut or rule of thumb that simplifies decision-making and problem-solving. Heuristics often speed up the process of finding a satisfactory solution, but they can also lead to cognitive biases" (Frimodig, 2023).

[19] Layperson: someone who is not an expert in or does not have a detailed knowledge of a particular subject (Cambridge Dictionary)

[20] "Grit is passion and perseverance for long-term goals" (Duckworth, 2023).

***<u>Change only comes from consistency, self-love, compassion, and self-discipline.</u>***

Secondly, you need to collect data.

***"Data! Data! Data! I can't make bricks without clay!"***

***– Arthur Conan Doyle (creator of Sherlock Homes)***

Fredrickson has a free website where you can track your practice of positivity (I will share it in the appendix of this book). I used this resource for over two weeks, and I was shocked at how my whole outlook on my life changed. I felt like the fog of negativity that had floated down over me had gradually dissipated. I began to look for more uplifting moments in my life again. I began to make my way back to the "glass half full" person that I always was.

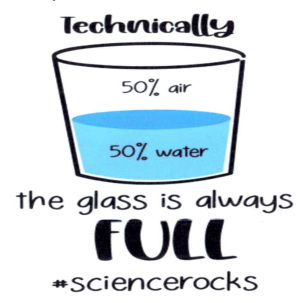

---

[21] Image: (Erin).

## Strive for M.O.R.E

At the beginning of this chapter, I mentioned perspective. Since we are prone to latch on to the negative, it may be time for another Wellbeing Waza that works great with the three good thoughts/events exercise. Since consistency is so important to change and changing our thought patterns, which can be difficult, this exercise might be a way for you to work on that.

*Wellbeing Waza:*

## "BUILD A POSITIVITY PORTFOLIO!"

Before you begin this project, let's talk about what positive emotions are, ok? There is more to positivity than just being *happy* or *joyful*. Fredrickson suggests that there are ten positive emotions. Here's the list:

1 – Joy   2 – Gratitude   3 – Inspiration

4 – Pride   5 – Interest   6 – Awe

7 – Serenity   8 – Hope   9 – Amusement

10 – Love

To create a positive emotions portfolio, you can make it simple or as complex as you like. What I mean by that is you can do something as simple as set up folders/albums on your phone and put pictures in each or create an actual physical scrapbook with items, images, etc. that relate to the various emotions. I have albums on my phone labeled with the above emotions and have put pictures in them that speak to me. Here are a couple of them:

## Strive for M.O.R.E

### Awe

### Serenity

## Pride

You are probably wondering, how is this supposed to make me more positive? We are our thoughts. When we dwell on the negative, we *are* more negative. Having a source of positive emotions/thoughts at the ready is a great way to quickly balance out the negative you may be experiencing. Once you have these portfolios done, engage with them regularly. Here's a great idea... instead of scrolling through your social media accounts, look at your portfolios! There are numerous studies suggesting that social media can lead to depressive thoughts and tendencies (Karim, 2020; Odgers, 2020). Staying away from social media should really be a Wellbeing Waza, but I know that many people use different social platforms for communication and business promotion (me included). Social media can be a double-edged sword: good in some ways and horrible in others. I will say that the research I have read on social media has consistently shown it to be psychologically bad, especially in younger users. From a career martial artist's perspective, good self-esteem acts as a shield for many of the negative and questionable posts that can be seen on social media. Additionally, when you put yourself out there and post, and the response is less than favorable, higher self-esteem can buffer the effects. Building self-esteem only comes from trying things outside your comfort zone. When self-esteem is built in this way – **_no one_** can take it away from you!

Back briefly to social media and why it took off like wildfire: We are social creatures. Even if you are a hardcore introvert like me, you do need interaction and connection with others. This leads us to the next pillar – relationships.

# RELATIONSHIPS

*(stock image)*

***"A human being is part of a whole, called by us the "Universe," a part limited in time and space. He experiences himself, his thoughts, and his feelings as something separated from the rest — a kind of optical delusion of his consciousness. This delusion is a kind of prison for us, restricting us to our personal desires and to affection for a few persons nearest us. Our task must be to free ourselves from this prison by widening our circles of compassion to embrace all living creatures and the whole of nature in its beauty."***

***- Albert Einstein.***

Well, we have made it to the "**R**" part of our quest to understand some of what the science shows makes us happier. I will say by this time, you should be looking at the word *happy* a bit differently. Let's do a quick recap of why. Happiness can be fleeting and intermittent. It depends on our circumstances and input from our environment, in addition to our own personal histories and genetics. *Flourishing* or *living a good life* is a better way to access or evaluate our lives. Make no mistake: you are the only one who can determine whether you are flourishing or living a good life. These are subjective terms, and we are talking about ***subjective*** well-being here!

On to relationships. Why did this make the short list? Earlier in this book, I mentioned one of the longest longitudinal studies[22] in history, *The Grant Study*, the name it started off with around 1937 – today it's referred to as the *Harvard Study of Adult Development.* While the study had several iterations and leaders, the vast amount of data gathered during this ongoing study suggests that good relationships are ***the*** most important aspect of a *good life*. What does that mean? First, let's dive into the study a bit.

I was unaware of the *Harvard Grant* or *Glueck* studies before reading the article *What Makes Us Happy* by Joshua Wolf Shenk (link included in the appendix if you want to read the article for yourself!). The first question I had right after learning of a study of this length, over eighty years, is what did the researchers learn? Well, they learned (and are continuing to learn)

---

[22] In a longitudinal study, researchers repeatedly examine the same individuals to detect any changes that might occur over a period of time. Longitudinal studies are a type of correlational research in which researchers observe and collect data on a number of variables without trying to influence those variables. While they are most commonly used in medicine, economics, and epidemiology, longitudinal studies can also be found in other social or medical sciences (Thomas, 2022).

A LOT! *The Harvard Grant Study* began in 1937 and was attempting to answer the question, "How can you live a long and happy life?" (Powell, 2012). The Harvard arm of the study had 268 male subjects who were deemed young and physically fit. They were *Harvard Men* and, at the time, were considered (here's where the bias of time and place can be seen) to be great subjects for a study to determine what makes up a good life. Hopefully, I don't have to explain that any further. W.T. Grant, whose name graced the study at the beginning, was a successful businessman who funded the study initially.

*The Harvard Grant Study* men were given extensive physical examinations and psychological evaluations and were subjected to interviews by social workers every two years for the duration of the research. Additionally, the subjects submitted questionnaires and narratives documenting all aspects of their lives, both physically and mentally. *The Harvard Grant Study* men were questioned about their careers, relationships, and habits – no stone was left unturned. To broaden the data gathered, researchers also interviewed the subjects' friends and family members. The team assembled was attempting to examine these lives in *real-time* and not rely on the subjects' memories as memory can be faulty.

*The Glueck Study* began as a study examining juvenile delinquency. The researchers, Sheldon and Eleanor Glueck, were criminologists at Harvard University and began their study with 456 young men from the inner city of Boston (Harvard Medical School and Massachusetts General Hospital, 2015). Unfortunately, *The Glueck Study* lost steam, and when George Vaillant took over *The Harvard Grant Study,* he breathed new life into the Glueck's research. Shenk shares, "In the 1970s, Vaillant and his staff tracked down most of the nondelinquent boys – it took years – so that today the *Harvard Study of Adult Development* consists of two cohorts, the 'Grant men' and the 'Glueck men'" (Shenk, 2009). Vaillant's decision to bring together these two groups enabled researchers to have two different perspectives: those whom one would assume their lives would be productive and full of success and happiness (Harvard men) and those who would struggle with every aspect – careers, health, and relationships (Glueck men).

In the article, *What Makes Us Happy*, Shenk shares some of his first impressions of this unprecedented access to the study material. He describes a large room with thousands of files, "The files holding the data are as thick as unabridged dictionaries" (Shenk, 2009). So, what *has* this research revealed? After reading the portion of Shenk's article where he wrote about the extensive physical exams the study subjects endured, I was expecting the outcomes to be related to controlling our cholesterol levels through diet or some aspect of physical fitness levels and how they relate to our long-term health. Not so. The revelations shared in Shenk's article, a TedTalk by Dr. Robert Waldinger (current study director – link to this Ted Talk in the appendix) and Vaillant's observations are surprisingly common sense related. The keys to living a long, happy, and successful life are relationships and love. WOW! I was blown away when I read that. It seems so simple. But is it?

What do the relationships Vaillant and Waldinger say are essential to wellbeing look like? The definition of "relationship" that is found in the Merriam-Webster dictionary states, "the way in which two or more people, groups, countries, etc., talk to, behave toward, and deal with each other." In doing some research about developing relationships, I came across both psychology-based references and contributions from those attempting to help folks relate better in their careers. Interestingly, the data was similar. The PhD who wrote the article for the psychology source I am including here suggests several ways in which we can improve our personal and intimate relationships.

Some of them include:

1. Get in touch with and understand the needs that affect your reactions and behaviors in a relationship.

2. Understand the fears that drive your reactions and behaviors.

3. Check whether your expectations are realistic.

4. Understand the messages that drive your interactions with your partner.

5. Be willing to take responsibility for your part in the problems and difficulties which arise between you and your partner.

6. Develop self-awareness (Gil, 2016).

On the business side of relationship building, experts suggest:

1. Develop your listening skills.

2. Embrace diversity.

3. Trust more.

4. Be able to give and take criticism.

5. Foster empathy (Freifeld, 2013).

Let's now unpack a few of these suggestions. I want to start with what I think should have probably been listed first with personal relationships, number six – develop self-awareness! What does it mean to be *self-aware*? The good news? We are already working on it here in this book. If you are showing up and doing the Wellbeing Wazas, then you are working on being more self-aware. The first ones we covered in the **MEANING** section were designed to get you in touch with *you*. We covered another suggestion when we talked about negativity bias and working on developing our positivity in the **OPTIMISM & POSITIVITY** section. In practicing the Wellbeing Wazas shared there, we are chipping away at number two – "understand the fears that drive your reactions and behaviors." See what I mean about the **M.O.R.E.** acronym and these foundations of well-being. They really do overlap! This is one thing I used to always share with my karate students, "When you practice one waza over and over again (Ren ma – polishing), that practice is never wasted as it supports many other aspects of your skills as a martial artist."

What I find stands out about both relationship building perspectives is these suggestions need to be executed by the individual. Simply put, they start from within. This leads me to something I've often heard on this path to understanding wellness/well-being: we must cultivate a good relationship with ourselves first. One TedTalk presenter said, "The relationship you have with yourself is the longest one you will ever have" (McGonigal, 2012). I truly believe this. If we cannot and do not love and understand ourselves, we will have great difficulty cultivating relationships, at least the kind that will bring us long-term health and well-being.

*I think it's time for another Wellbeing Waza:*

## "TAKE THE VIA CHARACTER STRENGTHS SURVEY!"

Here is another tool to cultivate a better relationship with yourself (develop self-awareness) and others. This survey was developed by Dr. Christopher Peterson, one of the founders of Positive Psychology. The VIA Character Strengths website shares the following about knowing and understanding your character strengths:

### Why Do Character Strengths Matter?

Character strengths are the positive parts of your personality that make you feel authentic and engaged. You possess all 24 character strengths in different degrees, giving you a unique character strengths profile. Research shows that understanding and applying your strengths can help:

- ❖ Boost Confidence
- ❖ Increase Happiness
- ❖ Strengthen Relationships
- ❖ Manage Problems
- ❖ Reduce Stress
- ❖ Accomplish Goals
- ❖ Build Meaning and Purpose

### ❖ Improve Work Performance

What's so great about this survey is that when you have taken it and get your results, you get a wonderful picture of *your* personal character strengths! You can then use this data in so many ways by applying the knowledge of these strengths in your daily life, both at home and in the workplace. Several additional resources allow you to take a deeper dive into your strengths if you choose. Again, one of these sources will be included in the appendix of this book. The survey takes about fifteen minutes to complete. Aren't you worth fifteen minutes? You betcha'!

Here's the link to the survey https://www.viacharacter.org/

Go for it! I'll see you on the other side.

*(stock image)*

So, how did you do? What are your top five?

Here's mine:

1 – Gratitude

2 – Appreciation of Beauty & Excellence

3 – Kindness

4 – Love of Learning

## 5 – Hope

Mine feels spot on. How about yours? Did you learn anything new about yourself? Can you think of ways to use your strengths on a daily basis? How about in your relationships? Sorry to bombard you with questions, but these tools are exciting to me! I want to point out that the VIA Character Strengths Survey is a bit different than the personality tests out there.

## *Invigorate Your Intellect*

***Personality Tests.***

"*A personality test aims to assess aspects of a person's character that remain stable across situations, referred to as their personality. Personality is generally understood as a collection of emotional, thought, and behavioral patterns unique to a person that is consistent over time. Generally, personality tests assess common characteristics for large segments of the population, describing people according to a number of dimensions or traits rather than attempting to describe every detail of any particular individual's personality.*

*Based on various approaches to the nature of personality, a variety of methods have been developed to assess personality differences and characteristics. While none are a complete description of human personality, many tests have proven useful in* specific applications, such as interviewing prospective employees, by focusing on the attributes important for the particular situation. Through this use, a good fit can be found between an individual and what they will be called on to accomplish, thus benefiting both the individual and the whole purpose they are serving.

*The Early History of Personality Testing:*

Greek philosopher Hippocrates recorded the first known personality model, basing his four "types" on the amount of body fluids, or "humors," an individual possessed. Greek physician Galen expounded upon Hippocrates' theory based on the four basic body fluids (humors): blood, phlegm, black bile, and yellow bile. According to their relative predominance in an individual, they would produce, respectively, temperaments designated sanguine (warm, pleasant), phlegmatic (slow-moving, apathetic), melancholic (depressed, sad), and choleric (quick to react, hot-tempered). German philosopher Immanuel Kant popularized these ideas by organizing the constructs along the two axes of **feelings** and **activity**.

The advent of the field of psychology led to more formalized categories and tests. For example, Wilhelm Wundt proposed that the four temperaments fall along the axes of changeability and emotionality.

*Varieties of personality assessment:*

As the field of psychology developed, so did the theories of personality and methods used to assess personality differences. A wide range of personality tests are available for use for a variety of purposes in different situations. The first personality test was the Woodworth Personal Data Sheet first used in 1919. It was designed to help the United States Army screen out recruits *who might be susceptible to shell shock"* (New World Encyclopedia, 2022).

*You may be familiar with some of them: Myers–Briggs Type Indicator, 16 Personality Factor, The Big Five, etc.*

*Many of these tests can be found online; some are free, and some are not. I recommend taking some of these too. It's both fun and educational.*

---

Getting back to the VIA Character Strengths – once you are familiar with your top five and your other nineteen strengths, try to look for them in those that are close to you. This can be a great way to see them in action by observing others (those whom you are close to are the best to start with since they are more familiar to you). When you see them in action in others, it can be easier to recognize them in yourself and make it easier to use your top five daily. Dr. Peterson and colleagues suggest that your top five should feel the most authentic to you.

I now want to circle back and talk briefly about the number four suggestion on the business side of how to build better relationships – "be able to give and take criticism." This is a tough one. I have noticed over the years folks are getting much more sensitive about… well, EVERYTHING! I've been thinking for a long time about why this is happening. Maybe it's due to the pandemic and increased levels of uncertainty and stress. Maybe it's down to folks not finding and using good outlets for stress – e.g., exercise, getting out in nature, meditation? There are so many more possibilities. One thing I do know is that we all take things *WAY* too personally. During the height of my karate career, we had to spar (fight) with fellow students daily. Over my tenure, I figure that I have probably fought over 10,000 rounds. One of the many lessons that I learned was as soon as you let your emotions get the best of you while sparring, you lose. In other words, you can't get emotional while sparring! What triggers our emotions? So many things. Mostly our past experiences and upbringing (Abramowitz & Berenbaum, 2007; Bynum, *et al.*,2019; Caldara, *et al.,*2017). Frankly, this is a topic for another book. Ha! Let me go back to sparring again. One needs to practice detachment when sparring, keeping emotions at bay. I used to tell my students, "When you get hit while sparring, you can't take it personally! Additionally, you are not a mind reader. There's no way to know what is going on in your opponent's mind. You don't know what they are bringing to the sparring match." We can only experience the world through our own lenses. *All* of our experiences are inside us. When trying to build better relationships, we need to practice compassion and empathy.

Compassion and empathy are not the same. The dictionary shares, "What is the difference between empathy and compassion? Compassion and empathy both refer to a caring response to someone else's distress. While empathy refers to an active sharing in the emotional experience of the other person, compassion adds to that emotional experience a desire to alleviate the person's distress" (Merriam-Webster Dictionary, 2023). If you read the above carefully, it suggests that we need to go outside ourselves and see things from someone else's point of view – "an active sharing in the emotional experience of the other person." So, ***practicing*** (there's that word again – ***practice***!) empathy and compassion will allow you to take things less personally. You will be working on being able to take and in turn provide criticism. I actually like the term *feedback* better, it's a little less harsh. So how do I practice compassion and empathy? I'm so glad you asked... It's time for another Wellbeing Waza!

*Wellbeing Waza:*

## "LOVING-KINDNESS MEDITATION"

This is a great meditation to practice. I know I have not shared anything about mediation so far in this book, sorry! It has been my experience over many years of teaching meditation classes that people can have a very hard time meditating. It is hard. What I'm suggesting here is a great way to develop compassion and understanding and frankly gain more joy from within. This meditation dates to early Buddhism. "Loving-kindness, also known as *metta* (in Pali), is derived from Buddhism and refers to a mental state of unselfish and unconditional kindness to all beings" (Hofmann, 2011). It only takes about ten to fifteen minutes. We **all** have ten to fifteen minutes to invest in our well-being!

Here's what to do:

Find a quiet place where you will not be disturbed. I have included this beautiful image to get you in the mood to relax and unwind!

*(stock image)*

Close your eyes and take some deep breaths. Try to relax your body a bit. I don't recommend lying down for this meditation as you don't want to fall asleep. Picture someone you love deeply in your mind (you can picture your furry family members, too!). Focus on your heart region and take a moment to get in touch with the emotions that come up about who you are picturing.

*(stock image)*

While continuing to picture your loved one, silently repeat the following phrases in your mind:

**May you be safe.**

**May you be happy.**

**May you be healthy.**

**May you live with ease.**

After a few moments of repeating these phrases and thinking about your loved one, shift your focus to someone you come in contact with regularly – maybe a colleague or someone at your gym, etc. Take a moment to visualize that person and then repeat silently in your mind the same phrases:

**May you be safe.**

**May you be happy.**

**May you be healthy.**

**May you live with ease.**

Shift your focus once again after a few moments and picture someone you don't care for.

*You can make yourself the focus if you are having thoughts of low self-worth.* Visualize this person as clearly as you can in your mind. You can also visualize a group of folks that you are a part of or even the world as a whole. You get the drift (I hope). Then again, repeat the same phrases:

**May you be safe.**

**May you be happy.**

**May you be healthy.**

**May you live with ease.**

To end the practice, take a few deep breaths, give yourself a moment to return to where you are sitting, and then slowly open your eyes. Continue this practice for at least two weeks and assess how you feel. It's great when beginning a meditation practice to take some notes. As always, journaling is optional if it seems tedious to you!

Everyone I have shared this loving-kindness meditation with has told me they feel so much better even after a week of doing it. These are the folks who actually showed up and did it daily! Interestingly, there have been several studies carried out regarding meditation. Barbara Fredrickson put loving-kindness mediation to the test. Her study participants were from a large corporation. She was able to have both a control group[23] and an experimental group[24]. The results were eye-opening. Fredrickson shares, "The findings are clear cut: The practice of LKM [loving-kindness mediation] led to shifts in people's daily experiences of a wide range of positive emotions, including love, joy, gratitude, contentment, hope, pride, interest, amusement, and awe. These increases in positive emotions were evident both within the trajectories of change in daily emotions over the span of 9 weeks and within a detailed analysis of a given morning 2 weeks after formal training ended" (Fredrickson B. L., 2008). What I found in this study to back up what I have been saying here throughout this book (and my entire career in martial arts) is that consistency is key!

Let me say that again – ***CONSISTENCY IS KEY***!

Fredrickson and colleagues suggest that "intentional activity is required to sustain gains in happiness" (Fredrickson B. L., 2008). Additionally, she shares that the study participants reported a dip in their positive emotions at the beginning of the LKM practice and a tremendous increase as the study continued. When we take on something new, we will feel a lack of confidence to start with. This is what I referred to at the beginning of this book as breaking out of our comfort zones. Trust me, if you adopt this meditation practice, you WILL see a difference! Read the study for yourself.

---

[23] control group, the standard to which comparisons are made in an experiment (Godby, 2022).

[24] experimental group: (in an experiment or clinical trial) a group of subjects who are exposed to the variable under study ( Dictionary.com, 2023).

Back to building relationships with the people we are close to. Have you ever thought about what if those who were close to you had never been in your life? Thinking about those close to you in this sort of way may seem counterintuitive but research suggests that it's actually not. Sonja Lyubomirsky wrote about a study in an article for *Scientific American*. She is a renowned happiness researcher, and some of her work is featured in the appendix of this book. Subjects in the study wrote about their spouse/significant other in one of two ways: how they met or what if they had never met. The results were interesting. Those who wrote about what if they had never met their spouse/significant other were actually happier. What?! Dr. Lyubomirsky shares, "The research showed that people prompted to write about how a positive event may *not* have happened experience a greater uptick in mood than those prompted to describe the positive event" (Lyubomirsky S., 2009). You can also do what the experimental group did, take 15 to 20 minutes and write about how your life would have been different if you didn't meet your significant other/spouse.

I have included a worksheet for you to use to get your thought process going. It's a bit different compared to what the study participants did, but I think it is still a very helpful tool. The worksheet I have included can be used for those close to you or colleagues, friends, etc. I suggest you use it to help you with the next Wellbeing Waza.

The questions included are designed to help you think deeply about the person you are trying to address for the worksheet. Think about what you love about that person. Consider what you would miss about them. Since there are always downsides to every relationship and person (that includes you and me!), think about what you want to embrace the most and what you want to remember about your relationship with them. It sounds easy, but trust me, it is not. We are erring on the side of positivity and choosing to throw away our negativity bias about this person and put them in the best light. Why? Well, compassion and empathy for one. We all deserve it.

Take a few minutes to look over the worksheet. If you like, you can print it out and use it to jot down your thoughts. Or you can just use a notepad with the person's name at the top and note your answers to the questions. Remember what I mentioned earlier about taking things too personally? Try to consider the person and the qualities they have that bring out the best in you. Enjoy!

# Strive for M.O.R.E

**Person In My Life:** _____

*What I love about you:*

*What I choose to embrace about you:*

*What I would miss about you:*

*What I want to remember about our relationship:*

Well, what did you think? I found it very thought-provoking and, frankly, a bit difficult.

When I was in school, I learned the most from the teachers whom I didn't like. They were the ones who challenged me. We once had an instructor at the karate school who lots of students didn't like. In fact, I was getting ready for class once, and there were four or five other women in the locker room who were changing back into their street clothes while I was putting on my gi (karate uniform). I asked where they were going, and they said, "We're leaving. We don't like who's teaching class tonight." I was saddened and shocked by this. This instructor was a very knowledgeable martial artist and a great practitioner. My response to them was, "The instructor is not here to win a popularity contest. Our job is to learn all we can, and this instructor knows a ton. If you leave, you will only be hurting your own training." They were taking it personally when it wasn't even personal! Some people come into our lives to help us grow, and growth can be painful sometimes. My grandmother used to call these people in our lives that help us grow "sandpaper." She said, "Jan, they help to smooth out your rough edges!"

Take the time to complete the worksheet for as many people as you would like to. Then, choose just one person. Someone that you are filled with gratitude to have in your life. This will lead us into the next Wellbeing Waza.

*Wellbeing Waza:*

## "THE GRATITUDE VISIT"

The Gratitude Visit was developed by Dr. Martin Seligman and his psychology students. What's great about this Wellbeing Waza is not only will your mood be lifted, but the person you choose for this exercise will get a boost, too. Here's what you need to do. Take the time to write down three hundred or so words about why you are grateful for this person. (See why I shared the previous worksheet with you first?!) I suggest writing it on nice paper or a card or getting creative as you are going to give this to the person when you meet with them next. Create your *gratitude visit gift* for them and then set the meeting. Don't tell them why you are meeting. Once you are at the get-together, read the words you have written for them out loud. I highly recommend bringing tissues, too! This is such a cathartic experience for both parties involved. Seligman's research suggests that those who participated in a Gratitude Visit had elevated moods for up to six months after the visit. I love this one! I don't know if you are like me, but I love to give gifts. As a matter of fact, I have a hard time waiting for the actual occasion for the gift. Much of the time, I give my gifts early simply because I can't wait. Give this one a try; you won't regret it!

If you are a manager or have people you work with closely, this is also a great way to express your gratitude. What a great way to build morale and help your employees grow. I promise you they will **NEVER** forget it. This type of activity goes way beyond the typical ways folks think will motivate people. A gratitude visit can be more valuable than a bonus or a raise. Give it a try!

Let's briefly recap this section on relationships. Great relationships start with making sure you have a solid relationship with yourself first. You must do this work – you *are* worth it. This is the highest form of self-care, much more valuable and long-lasting than a *spa day* or *happy hour*. Develop and practice compassion and empathy. Like Einstein said, *"widening our circles of compassion to embrace all living creatures and the whole of nature in its beauty."* Use your top five character strengths every day, and keep them where you can look at them regularly. Practice loving-kindness meditation daily.

On to our last section – **ENGAGEMENT.**

# **ENGAGEMENT**

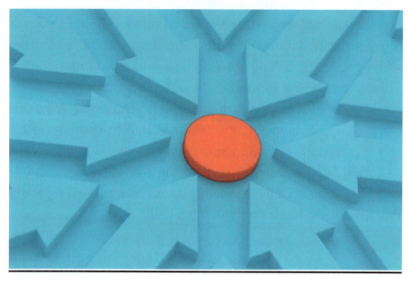

*(stock image)*

*"The best moments in our lives, are not the passive, receptive, relaxing times—although such experiences can also be enjoyable, if we have worked hard to attain them. The best moments usually occur when a person's body or mind is stretched to its limits in a voluntary effort to accomplish something difficult and worthwhile."*

*– Dr. Mihaly Csikszentmihalyi*

What is engagement? Some of you may have heard this term around the water cooler at work. Employers seem to talk a lot about engagement or the lack of it in the workplace. These are folks who are distracted at work and not *engaged*. Dr Mihaly Csikszentmihalyi (Me-high Chick-sent-me-high – I know, it's a tough one!) is one of Dr. Martin Seligman's colleagues and another important player in the Positive Psychology world. His work, beginning in the 1970s, led him to surmise that we are most happy when challenged by our own voluntary actions/activities. But what does *that* mean?

To unpack this a bit, we need to start by defining motivation. The dictionary defines motivation as "the reason or reasons one has for acting or behaving in a particular way" (Google Dictionary Box). Okay, we all seem to know this already. Now, I want to share the two types of motivation that I think are important here: extrinsic and intrinsic. Some of you may or may not be familiar with these terms. If you are, this will be a good refresher.

Briefly, extrinsic motivation is defined as "an external incentive to engage in a specific activity, especially motivation arising from the expectation of punishment or reward" (American Psychological Association, 2023). Most people understand this type of motivation. Beginning in childhood, we quickly learned that certain things we did we were either rewarded or punished for. There is much research to suggest that extrinsic motivation, specifically centered around money, does not work all that well. Harvard Business Review shares some findings from a meta-analysis[25] of one hundred and twenty years of research. The findings revealed – "the association between salary and job satisfaction is very weak" (Chamorro-Premuzic, 2013). Remember what I just mentioned in the last section about the Gratitude Visit with a colleague?

---

[25] "Meta-analysis is a statistical process that combines the data of multiple studies to find common results and to identify overall trends" (Tech & Science Dictionary, 2023).

Intrinsic motivation is defined as "an incentive to engage in a specific activity that derives from pleasure in the activity itself" (American Psychological Association, 2023). This is the motivation that is directly connected to engagement or *flow state*. We do something for the pure joy of it. Now, you might be thinking about all your potentially bad habits/interests and wondering, "I love doing *those* things. Do they count?" Nope. We all know what I'm talking about – too much scrolling, caffeine, alcohol, shopping, junk food, etc. This is definitely not a book that will give you the green light to go all in with these types of activities. What we *are* talking about are activities that challenge you just enough for you to keep at it and grow. Csikszentmihalyi is very specific; the *flow state* occurs during *active* pursuits, e.g., athletics, art, chess, and the like, not passive activities – watching television, scrolling, etc. (Csikszentmihalyi, 1996). Remember the definition of wellness from the very beginning of this journey – wellness is an "active pursuit."

Remember that I mentioned languishing at the beginning of this book? Well, Csikszentmihalyi's work can help us overcome this feeling, too. How? Languishing can make you feel like you don't want to do much of anything. You feel **stuck**. That's when you need to take some small steps. It's just like building the skills needed to find *flow* in activities we enjoy. We start small and show up regularly, and all of a sudden, we start to master what we are pursuing. Additionally, Csikszentmihalyi asserts that people who achieve a *flow state* do so not for money or recognition. Instead, they pursue these activities for the joy of the activity itself.

*"It's exhilarating to come closer and closer to self-discipline."*

*– Dr. Mihaly Csikszentmihalyi*

I love this quote! (You may have already guessed that!) This sentiment is what I have been sharing with people for my entire karate career. Self-discipline is **_good_**! There has been some scholarship to back up that self-disciplined people are happier (Hofmann W, 2014). Hofmann and colleagues found that study participants with higher self-control levels experienced less conflict. So why am I bringing up self-discipline when I'm supposed to be talking about engagement? Well, we have been spending this time together trying to unravel the science of wellbeing (and change, for that matter) and over and over again, we keep circling back to self-discipline. I say this a lot to folks I talk to, "Self-discipline is the *only* way to *any* success." Whether you are trying to live a better life, get a new job, lose weight, get in shape, find love, etc. – self-discipline is the key ingredient.

*Period*.

Onward with engagement and *flow state*. In the martial arts *flow state* is referred to as *mushin*. Mushin means *empty mind* or *no mind*. *Flow state* (or mushin) is one of the many benefits, in my experience, in the study and pursuit of martial arts. At the beginning of my karate training, I was unsure of myself. I was unfamiliar with the techniques (wazas!) I was being taught, and the etiquette. It's like any new pursuit when you are green. One of the reasons I was able to achieve *flow* or mushin was my ritual of practicing my techniques hundreds of times every day. I would practice at work when I went to the bathroom, at home morning and night, and in outdoor spaces near my home. All of these places were, of course, outside the dojo (training hall) and offered the opportunity for distraction. Yes, I said distraction. Distraction is good when you are trying to learn to focus. When there are distractions, you need to dig down deep to where your **grit** (remember I mentioned **grit** at the beginning of this voyage?) resides and ignore your desire to give in to the distractions.

## Strive for M.O.R.E

To some of you reading this, it may resonate with you; to others, it may be a head-scratcher.

In karate or empty-hand self-defense, it is very important for techniques to be second nature. By practicing or polishing (ren ma), the practitioner achieves mushin or *empty mind*. After I got my bearings, I was able to regularly lose myself in the training. Csikszentmihalyi suggests that when we are in *flow state* we lose track of time. I definitely experienced this daily while training. In fact, I used to tell students that karate is a form of moving meditation. I'm sure if you are an athlete, you have lost track of time while participating in your chosen activity. My yoga practice offered the same opportunity to achieve mushin. I believe I was able to excel in my yoga practice because I already understood empty mind. So, what does all of this mean for you if you are new to experiencing or haven't ever experienced *flow state* or mushin? Find something that challenges you, but you still enjoy doing! Sounds simple, right? There can be plenty of trial and error when trying to find something where you can experience *flow*. Csikszentmihalyi suggests that you can even achieve *flow* in everyday activities. I will say that I have lost track of time while cleaning. How about you? Have you lost track of time while doing something? (Something that falls within Csikszentmihalyi's suggestion of "active pursuits"). As many of us have experienced, scrolling can suck you into a vortex and suddenly, hours have flown by. That's why social media experts design these platforms that way. Don't get sucked in by them!

When you are looking for that activity that will allow you to get into a *flow state*, you will experience failure – lots of it. We seem to have been taught that failure is bad. Think about extrinsic motivation – "expectation of punishment or reward." I know I said earlier about our experiences and how they shape us, that some may be caught up in their past and be fearful of failure. It's important not to fear failure. Instead, learn to embrace it and grow. I hope you are not getting the impression that my karate training was not without its pitfalls. There were many times when I wanted to quit. I would sit in the parking lot in my car before class, grip the steering wheel, breathe deep, and tell myself, "You can do this." There's that pesky comfort zone I had to move out of!

Another very important element to *flow* is goal setting. Csikszentmihalyi suggests that activities where we can achieve *flow state* have goals. I'm not going to get into a deep discussion about goal setting, as that has become an entire industry. I would hope that people understand goals and goal setting at least to a certain degree. Hopefully, you are starting to picture in your mind what I'm trying to share with you here. Find an activity – sport, hobby, game, etc. – that you think you might enjoy, set a goal, and get at it. Know you *will* fail – possibly A LOT. Learn from those failures. Practice and improve your skills. Practice some more. And then practice some more again. Achieve your goals and then set new goals.

I think the environment and etiquette at a dojo is why it can be so easy to achieve *flow* or mushin. In the beginning, many aspects of training are strange, from having to wear a gi (karate uniform) and being barefoot to understanding the structure of the hierarchy, to the use of Japanese terminology during class and so on. All facets of a new experience can definitely take one out of their comfort zone. *Flow state* also happens when there is a degree of risk involved in the activity. When you are out of your comfort zone, you are forced to be more focused in the moment. You can't slip into Kahneman's *System 1* part of our brains. Instead, you must use *System 2*, the rational, logical, slower, effortful, conscious part that allows us to make complex decisions.

# Strive for M.O.R.E

This pillar is a tough one for a Wellbeing Waza. I can't really choose an activity for you that will allow you to step into mushin; you have to do your own research to achieve it. What I **can** do is make some suggestions that might help you on your path to reaching *flow state*. First, start with spending less time on your devices. I know, I know, that's a tough one for some of you. Some may even be feeling anxious and itchy just at the mere mention of putting down their devices! Trust me, you CAN do it. I'm not saying that you must stop using them altogether; just set time limits on their use. *Parents, this is VERY important for you and your children – remember, children learn from the models we give them! I'm not going to get bogged down in sharing the numerous studies that have been done relating to the use of social media and electronic devices. We've all heard it. Think about it this way: science has proven repeatedly that smoking is bad for our health, and yet people *still* smoke! Change is hard, and we all hate it, but we are meant to do hard things and grow. Another thing my grandmother used to say all the time to me was, "Change is the **only** thing you can count on." Another suggestion I would have to help you move closer to the *flow state* is to spend more time in nature. I know you may have heard this from others already. And they're spot on. When I say "spend more time in nature," I mean really take it in. Close your eyes and listen to the sounds you hear, breathe in deeply and smell the air, look up and take in the clouds in the sky. Be present. You get the drift. Some of you may be thinking, "I don't live near anywhere where there is *nature*." To some of you reading that last sentence, you may be scratching your head, but some of us do live in urban areas with limited

*(stock image)*

amounts of *nature*. Or the *nature* that is close by may even be dangerous – e.g., some city parks. I know you can find a way to get out there, though. Be safe and find a place that has trees and wildlife.

## LET'S WRAP IT ALL UP

Well, what have we learned? A LOT, I hope! You will have to figure out for yourself what stood out the most to you from our time together. That's what is so great *and* not so great about truly trying to understand wellbeing – it's complex and subjective, which makes it even *more* complex! My goal here was to give you a small glimpse into the oodles and oodles of research that has been done (and still being done) surrounding this topic. Frankly, I don't think anyone can completely understand it all. But I'm confident to say that the sources I've shared here (and in the appendix) are solid. One thing during my academic studies I learned you must know who is reliable in your field of study. There are many folks studying wellness and wellbeing – with some legit, and others not so legit.

What we have covered here will make a difference in your life if you show up and do the work. You're probably pretty sick of me saying that. Sorry, it's the truth. The first pillar, MEANING, comes from within us. What is meaningful to *you*? When we explored OPTIMISM & POSITIVE EMOTIONS, we never pointed fingers at anyone else. It was all about how *we* think, interpret, and feel about what is going on around us. The best part of learning about optimism and positivity was that we have the power to transform *how* we think and feel. It just takes practice! Remember what the experts recommended for building better relationships? *ALL* their suggestions started with the individual – you (and me!). *We* are the key to better relationships. Stop blaming everything on the *other person*. And finally, during our examination of ENGAGEMENT, the most important facet was to be present. Challenge yourself in ways you never thought possible, push out of your comfort zone, and take it all in.

*(stock image)*

*"If you want success, the foremost thing is to ensure that you are not the obstacle to it."*

***- Sadhguru***

I practice all of the Wellbeing Wazas I have shared here. I have had great success with them and continue to use them regularly. Is my life *perfect*? Nope, not even close. Am I more joyful, optimistic, and grateful? You bet. Living a life well lived doesn't mean there aren't bad times, tragedies, or difficulties. Understanding what the science shows really works and practicing those Wellbeing Wazas daily builds my resilience and GRIT (and they will build yours, too!) so I can better handle the pitfalls that come along.

Let's now put what I've shared into a short bullet list:

1) Wellness and wellbeing are active processes.

2) There are pillars or areas of our lives that we can/should focus on.

   a. **ME**ANING

   b. **O**PTIMISM and/or POSITIVE EMOTIONS

   c. **RE**LATIONSHIPS

   d. **E**NGAGEMENT

3) Showing up every day and doing *the work* is the **only** way to succeed.

4) Using the educational process is the **best** form of self-care!

5) Improving our lives is within our power, and there are evidence-based activities that really work!

We humans always gravitate toward the *easy* way. You see it all around us. We want quick fixes for everything. Get rich with only these few steps: five minutes to great abdominals, take this pill and lose those unwanted pounds, and on and on and on. I read something interesting the other day, the article suggested that our attention span is only about 6 seconds – 6 SECONDS!! WOW!! Let that sink in for a moment.

Wellbeing is vital to us all. Understanding wellness incorporates abstract ideas and phenomena intertwined with personal culture, tradition, psychological themes, and evidence-based research. Wellness is an active process, and it's subjective. I believe ***everyone*** is capable of living their best life.

So, now that we've explored some of the science related to wellbeing and some of the areas to work on, I think it's important to share the larger picture of why we so desperately need to bolster our personal wellbeing and self-care. It's onto the scary reality we find ourselves in today.

Strive for M.O.R.E

Here are five sobering statistics for you:

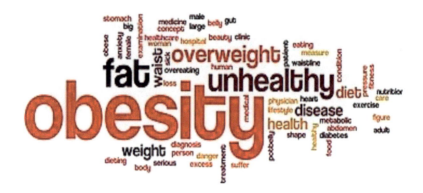

*(stock image)*

1) Obesity rates in the United States are at an all-time high – **41.9%** according to the CDC (Centers for Disease Control and Prevention, 2022). **Almost 1/2** of American adults are considered obese. Obesity is directly linked to lifestyle diseases which in turn have caused a surge in healthcare costs resulting in **$173 BILLION** spent in the United States in 2019 on medical costs related to obesity.

*(stock image)*

2) The use of antidepressant medication has been on the rise, too.

Use of these medications among those 12 years of age and up has increased by nearly **400 PERCENT** since 1988, according to Harvard Health Publishing (Wehrwein, 2011). While this article was written over ten years ago, there is still some weight to it. I found it interesting that the author mentioned that mental illness, specifically depression, had been underdiagnosed, but we can't ignore the marketing that pharmaceutical companies have done.

*(stock image)*

3) Divorce rates in the United States are around **40-50%** for first-time marriages. The rate increases with the second and third try at it – **60%** and **70%,** respectively (World Population Review, 2023). While overall, the rate of folks marrying has gone down, these statistics are still alarming.

*(stock image)*

4) Productivity losses due to health-related issues have had a substantial economic impact on businesses. Experts share that employee health-related absence, which contributes to decreased productivity, has an average annual economic loss of approximately 225.8 BILLION dollars. According to the Bureau of Labor and Statistics, in January 2022, **7.8 million** folks were out sick from work. That's **110%** more people than were out sick in January 2021! The **$225.8 billion** loss incurred due to these absences is more than business owners spend on their direct medical expenditures (U.S. Bureau of Labor Statistics, 2022). **<u>WOW!</u>**

(stock image)

5) In a new survey about anger and incivility in the workplace, the

Harvard Business Review collected data from over 2,000 people in more than 25 industries in various roles across the globe (representing every major region except Antarctica). They included both frontline employees and people who had observed them at work. Here's what the data revealed:

- 76% of respondents experience incivility at least once a month.

- 78% witness incivility at work at least once a month, and 70% witness it at least two to three times a month.

- 73% report that it's not unusual for customers to behave badly.

- 78% believe that bad behavior from customers toward employees is more common than it was five years ago.

- 66% believe bad behavior from customers toward other customers is more common than it was five years ago (Harvard Business Review, 2022).

**These figures paint a bleak picture. However, there is hope.**

*(stock image)*

Incorporating some of what I have shared with you in this book can have an impact. If each one of us takes responsibility for our own wellbeing that can have a ***huge*** impact on the world. Think about it for a moment. If you start to feel better about your life, your interactions with others improve, you set an example for your kids (if you have some!), you might even get a raise or a better job, and you will be more successful, happier, and grateful – the possibilities are now ***endless***! I think we've all heard of the ripple effect – a gradually spreading influence or series of consequences caused by a single action or event. If we all take charge of our wellbeing it will have a *ripple effect*. I know, I know, I have lofty ideas and a great imagination. But I truly believe that those who make a shift in how they think, act, and feel can at least create waves within their own circle.

# Strive for M.O.R.E

*(stock image)*

***"Just as ripples spread out when a single pebble is dropped into water, the actions of individuals can have far-reaching effects."***

*– Dalai Lama*

Now's the time to retake that test from the very beginning of this adventure! I have included it again here so you don't have to go back to the beginning:

## The Flourishing Scale

This is a brief **8**-item assessment used to measure the respondent's self-perceived success in important areas such as relationships, self-esteem, purpose, and optimism. The scale provides a psychological well-being score (Diener, et.al., 2009).

Below are **8** statements with which you may agree or disagree. Using the **1–7** scale below, indicate your level of agreement with each statement.

**Scale:**

1 - Strongly disagree

2 - Disagree

3 - Slightly disagree

4 - Mixed or neither agree nor disagree

5 - Slightly agree

6 - Agree

7 - Strongly agree

**Statements:**

1 - I lead a purposeful and meaningful life

2 - My social relationships are supportive and rewarding

3 - I am engaged and interested in my daily activities

4 - I actively contribute to the happiness and well-being of others

5 - I am competent and capable in the activities that are important to me

6 - I am a good person and live a good life

7 - I am optimistic about my future

8 - People respect me

Scoring: Add the responses, varying from **1** to **7**, for all eight items. The lowest possible score is **8**, while the highest is **56**.

\*\*\*A high score represents a person with many psychological resources and strengths.

Has your number changed? Hopefully it has. Remember our definition of wellness, "**an *active* process**." This means it is ongoing. How great is that? We get multiple chances to achieve our goals.

I would not be a responsible wellness/wellbeing educator if I did not include some information regarding how to improve physical health. This book was intended to explore and incorporate some of the research that's out there in regard to how we can improve our subjective wellbeing. When we engage in practices that lift our mood and our perception of our lives, the state of our physical health improves (Diener et al, 2017; Doan, et al., 2022; Sears, 2013). To conclude, here we go with some very basic information, some of which I *know* you have heard before.

*(stock image)*

Lifestyle diseases, such as type 2 diabetes, heart disease, and some cancers, *can* be prevented with changes to diet, exercise levels, improving the amount of sleep one gets, stress management, and the like. I know we have all heard this before from *many* different sources (very legitimate sources, I might add!). It makes me wonder about the obesity rates I mentioned earlier. It's shocking to hear in the United States those rates have gone from **30.5%** (1999-2000), over **70 MILLION** adults, to **41.9%** (2017-2020)! That's more than **108 MILLION** *obese* adults (Centers for Disease Control and Prevention, 2022). Is it that we don't care about our health? I hope not. Or is it that we've been seduced by the food industry and its great marketing and manufacturing techniques that make some foods sooooo addictive. Unfortunately, most Americans are consuming the Standard American Diet – ironically known as **S-A-D** or *sad*. SAD consists of animal products, refined grains, fats, and sugar and is low in whole grains, fruits, and vegetables (Forks Over Knives, 2016). The Standard American Diet has made lifestyle disease prevention elusive. I have encouraged many folks to switch to a whole food plant-based diet (WFPB) with tremendous success. By doing so I have seen people reverse health issues, lose weight, and improve their vitality. One of the dominant ideologies surrounding nutrition suggests that consuming animal products is essential for good health. However, there is an ever-growing body of scientific evidence that clearly illustrates that the consumption of a plant-based diet lowers the risk of chronic diseases (Kim, 2019). Additionally, plant-based diets have been shown to be environmentally sustainable and support a growing ideology of compassion regarding **animal welfare**. Oxford recently released a study vis-à-vis eating a plant-based diet – they concluded it is *the* single most effective way to have an impact on our environment (Clarka, 2019). I would add that not only does it impact our external environment, but our internal environment as well.

There are so many awesome resources to help with this kind of lifestyle change and over fifty years of research to back it up! Again, informing folks about diet is not my objective here.

> *"Let food be thy medicine."*
>
> *- Hypocrites*

In addition to a poor diet, few people participate in the recommended thirty minutes of daily physical activity shared by the Office of Disease Prevention and Health Promotion (2023). I get that not everyone loves to exercise, but I believe that we need to shift the way we think about it. What I mean is that most folks think they need to go to a gym, work out for hours, and feel sore afterward. That is not how it has to be. Our bodies were designed for movement, and that's what we should do with them – move them! Walking, especially walking out in nature, not only improves our physical health but has also been shown to elevate our mood (Grassini, 2022; Han et al., 2021; Pearce et al.,2022). Additionally, some of the research suggests just a minimal amount of walking can have maximum benefits. I don't want to get into this too deeply here, as educating folks about the benefits of exercise/movement is also not my intention with this book. However, we did talk about ENGAGEMENT and that underpinning of our wellbeing urges us to challenge ourselves in new ways (many of them physically) and work toward achieving mastery.

So, what are some things we can do today to start making those shifts? Utilizing the Wellbeing Wazas that I have shared here is a ***great*** place to start! As far as changing or working toward changing what's on your plate – take it one day at a time. And exercise? Just put one foot in front of the other and… ***be CONSISTENT!***

I didn't really talk too much about goal setting in this book. There are more than enough folks out there that have books they have written, courses they teach, and so on for that. I have mentioned to you ***numerous*** times throughout this text (ad nauseum frankly!) about self-discipline and its connection to success. I will connect it again here to goal setting. It's not enough to have a goal; you must have a plan that *you* can stick to, and then you actually need to stick to it! You must determine your MEANING (here's another overlap with striving for **M.O.R.E.!**).

What is your ***WHY***? This question is perhaps one of the most important to ask yourself when you are considering your goals. Make sure it is something very meaningful to you and something you can use to get you through those days when you want to stray from the plan to achieve your goals.

*(stock image)*

***"Really, what matters in the long run is sticking with things and working daily to get better at them."***

*– Angela Duckworth*

Wellness matters. Everything we do, every emotion we feel relates to our wellbeing. Moreover, our wellbeing directly shapes our actions and our emotions. Wellness and wellbeing require an endless cycle of action and reaction. Additionally, our ability to deeply understand the dimensions and pillars of wellness and wellbeing are fundamental to living a higher quality of life. Take time to gain an understanding of wellbeing – push outside your comfort zone. Optimize your emotional, spiritual, and physical wellness. It is not only significant for you as an individual, but the impact can also be widespread.

**Thank you! And be well.**

## APPENDIX

***Recommended Reading:***

**Martin E.P. Seligman books:**

*Flourish: A visionary new understanding of happiness and well-being.* 2011. Simon & Schuster.

*Authentic happiness: Using the new positive psychology to realize your potential for lasting fulfillment.* 2004. Simon & Schuster.

**Barbara Fredrickson books:**

*Positivity: Groundbreaking research reveals how to embrace the hidden strength of positive emotions, overcome negativity, and thrive.* 2009. Crown Publishers/Random House.

*Love 2.0: creating happiness and health in moments of connection.* 2013. Penguin Publishing Group.

*Website:* [https://www.positivityresonance.com/](https://www.positivityresonance.com/)

**Sonja Lyubomirsky books:**

*The How of Happiness: A New Approach to Getting the Life You Want.* 2008. Penguin Press.

*The Myths of Happiness: What Should Make You Happy, but Doesn't, What Shouldn't Make You Happy, but Does.* 2014. Penguin Publishing Group.

**Angela Duckworth book:**

*Grit: The Power of Passion and Perseverance.* 2016. Simon & Schuster.

**Mihaly Csikszentmihalyi book:**

*Flow: The Psychology of Optimal Experience.* 2008. Harper Perennial Modern Classics.

**Ed Diener book:**

*Happiness: Unlocking the Mysteries of Psychological Wealth*. 2008. Blackwell Publishing.

**Daniel Kahneman book:**

*Thinking, Fast and Slow*. 2011. Farrar, Straus and Giroux.

**Dan Buettner book:**

*The Blue Zones, Second Edition: 9 Lessons for Living Longer From the People Who've Lived the Longest*. 2012. National Geographic.

**VIA Character Strengths book:**

*The Power of Character Strengths: Appreciate and Ignite Your Positive Personality*. Authors: Ryan Niemiec and Bob McGrath. 2019. VIA Institute on Character.

**John W. Creswell and J. David Creswell book:**

*Research Design: Qualitative, Quantitative, and Mixed Methods Approaches 5th Edition*. 2018. Sage Publications.

**Harvard Study of Adult Development:**

https://www.theatlantic.com/magazine/archive/2009/06/what-makes-us-happy/307439/

https://www.ted.com/talks/robert_waldinger_what_makes_a_good_life_lessons_from_the_longest_study_on_happiness/c

## WORKS CITED

Dictionary.com. (2023). *experimental group.* Retrieved from Dictionary.com: https://www.dictionary.com/browse/experimental-group

(https://www.csupueblo.edu/health-education-and-prevention/8-dimension-of-well-being.html).8 Dimensions of Well-being. *Health Education & Prevention.* Colorado State University Pueblo, Pueblo, CO.

Abramowitz, A., & Berenbaum, H. (2007). Emotional triggers and their relation to impulsive and compulsive psychopathology. *Personality and Individual Differences*, 1356-1365.

American Psychological Association. (2023). *extrinsic motivation.* Retrieved from APA Dictionary of Psychology: https://dictionary.apa.org/extrinsic-motivation

American Psychological Association. (2023). *intrinsic motivation.* Retrieved from APA Dictionary of Psychology: https://dictionary.apa.org/intrinsic-motivation

American Psychological Association. (2023). *languishing.* Retrieved from APA Dictionary of Psychology: https://dictionary.apa.org/languishing

Bates, T. C. (2015, November 1). The Glass is Half Full and Half Empty: A population-representative twin study testing if Optimism and Pessimism are distinct systems. *J Posit Psychol*, pp. 533-542.

Bhandari, P. (2020, October 10). *What Is Qualitative Research? | Methods & Examples.* Retrieved from Scribbr: https://www.scribbr.com/methodology/qualitative-research/

*Brass ring.* (2022, October 22). Retrieved from Wikipedia: https://en.wikipedia.org/wiki/Brass_ring

Brown NJ, S. A. (2013). The complex dynamics of wishful thinking: the critical positivity ratio. *American Psychologist* , https://physics.nyu.edu/sokal/complex_dynamics_final_clean.pdf.

Buettner, D. (2012). *The Blue Zones, Second Edition: 9 Lessons for Living Longer From the People Who've Lived the Longest.* National Geographic.

Bynum, W. E., Artino, A. R., Uijtdehaage, S. P., Webb, A. M., & Varpio, L. P. (2019). Sentinel Emotional Events: The Nature, Triggers, and Effects of Shame Experiences in Medical Residents. . *Academic Medicine*, 85-93.

Caldara M, M. M. (2017). A Study of the Triggers of Conflict and Emotional Reactions. *Games*, 1-12.

Cambridge Dictionary. (n.d.). *layperson.* Retrieved from https://dictionary.cambridge.org/: https://dictionary.cambridge.org/dictionary/english/layperson

Catalyst, C. (n.d.). *Thinking Fast and Slow.* Germany.

Centers for Disease Control and Prevention. (2022, May 17). *Adult Obesity Facts.* Retrieved from https://www.cdc.gov/: https://www.cdc.gov/obesity/data/adult.html

Chamorro-Premuzic, T. (2013, April 10). *Does Money Really Affect Motivation? A Review of the Research.* Retrieved from https://hbr.org: https://hbr.org/2013/04/does-money-really-affect-motiv

Clarka, M. A. (2019, October 28). *Multiple health and environmental impacts of foods.* Retrieved from PNAS.org: https://www.pnas.org/doi/10.1073/pnas.1906908116#sec-2

Cleveland Clinic. (2022, June 6). *Parasympathetic Nervous System (PSNS)*. Retrieved from https://my.clevelandclinic.org/: https://my.clevelandclinic.org/health/body/23266-parasympathetic-nervous-system-psns#:~:text=Your%20parasympathetic%20nervous%20system%20is,you%20feel%20safe%20and%20relaxed.

Cox, D. A. (2022, March 24). *Generation Z and the Future of Faith in America.* Retrieved from Survey Center of American Life: https://www.americansurveycenter.org/research/generation-z-future-of-faith/#_edn1

Csikszentmihalyi, M. (1996). *Creativity: Flow and the psychology of discovery and invention.* New York: Harper Collins.

Diener, E. P.-C. (2017). If, Why, and When Subjective Well-Being Influences Health, and Future Needed Research. *Applied Psychology: Health and Well-Being*, 133-167.

Diener, E. W.-P.-D. (2009). Flourishing scale. *Social Indicators Research*, 247-266.

Doan, T. H. (2022). Healthy minds live in healthy bodies – effect of physical health on mental health: Evidence from Australian longitudinal data. *Current Psychology*, https://doi.org/10.1007/s12144-022-03053-7.

Duckworth, A. (2023). *FAQ.* Retrieved from Angela Duckworth: https://angeladuckworth.com/qa/

Erin. (n.d.). *SCIENCE ROCKS GLASS HALF FULL FREE SVG FILES 1684.* Free SVG Designs, https://freesvgdesigns.com/science-rocks-glass-half-full-free-svg-files-1684/.

Forks Over Knives. (2016, May 23). *The Standard American Diet is Even Sadder Than We Thought.* Retrieved from Forks Over Knives: https://www.forksoverknives.com/wellness/standard-american-diet-sadder-than-we-thought/

Fredrickson, B. (2009). *Positivity.* New York: Penguin Random House LLC.

Fredrickson, B. (2011, June 21). *Are You Getting Enough Positivity in Your Diet?* Retrieved from greatergood.berkeley.edu: https://greatergood.berkeley.edu/article/item/are_you_getting_enough_positivity_in_your_diet

Fredrickson, B. L. (2008). Open Hearts Build Lives: Positive Emotions, Induced Through Loving-Kindness Meditation, Build Consequential Personal Resources. *Journal of personality and social psychology*, 1-34.

Freifeld, L. (2013, March 21). *8 TIPS FOR DEVELOPING POSITIVE RELATIONSHIPS.* Retrieved from https://trainingmag.com: https://trainingmag.com/content/8-tips-developing-positive-relationships

Frimodig, B. (2023, July 10). *Heuristics: Definition, Examples, And How They Work.* Retrieved from Simply Psychology: https://www.simplypsychology.org/what-is-a-heuristic.html

Gil, D. (2016, July 17). *7 Tips on Developing and Maintaining a Successful Intimate Relationship.* Retrieved from http://psychcentral.com/: http://psychcentral.com/lib/7-tips-on-developing-and-maintaining-a-successful-intimate-relationship/

Gilbert, D. (2004). The surprising science of happiness. *https://www.ted.com/talks/dan_gilbert_the_surprising_science_of_happiness.* Monterey California: TedTalk.

Godby, M. E. (2022, October 28). *control group.* Retrieved from Encyclopedia Britannica: https://www.britannica.com/science/control-group

Google Dictionary Box. (n.d.). *mo·ti·va·tion.* Retrieved from Google.

Grassini, S. (2022). A Systematic Review and Meta-Analysis of Nature Walk as an Intervention for Anxiety and Depression. *Journal of clinical medicine*, https://doi.org/10.3390/jcm11061731.

Han A, K. J. (2021). A Study of Leisure Walking Intensity Levels on Mental Health and Health Perception of Older Adults. *Gerontology and Geriatric Medicine*, doi:10.1177/2333721421999316.

Harvard Business Review. (2022, November 9). *Frontline Work When Everyone Is Angry.* Retrieved from Harvard Business Review: https://hbr.org/2022/11/frontline-work-when-everyone-is-angry

Harvard Medical School and Massachusetts General Hospital. (2015). *STUDY OF ADULT DEVELOPMENT.* Retrieved from http://www.adultdevelopmentstudy.org/: http://www.adultdevelopmentstudy.org/grantandglueckstudy

Helmenstine, A. M. (2019, November 29). *What Is the Difference Between Hard and Soft Science?* Retrieved from ThoughtCo: https://www.thoughtco.com/hard-vs-soft-science-3975989

Hofmann W, L. M. (2014). Yes, but are they happy? Effects of trait self-control on affective well-being and life satisfaction. *Journal of Personality*, 265-77.

Hofmann, S. G. (2011, July 26). *Loving-Kindness and Compassion Meditation: Potential for Psychological Interventions.* Retrieved from National Library of Medicine: https://www.ncbi.nlm.nih.gov/pmc/articles/PMC3176989/

Kahneman, D. (2011). *Thinking Fast and Slow.* New York: Farrar, Stratus and Giroux.

Karim, F. O. (2020, June 15). *Social Media Use and Its Connection to Mental Health: A Systematic Review.* Retrieved from https://www.ncbi.nlm.nih.gov/: https://www.ncbi.nlm.nih.gov/pmc/articles/PMC7364393/

Kashdan, T. B. (2015, August 19). *What Really Makes You a Happy Person? :The experts say we only control 40 percent of our happiness. Are they right?* Retrieved from Psychology Today: https://www.psychologytoday.com/ca/blog/curious/201508/what-really-makes-you-happy-person

Kim, H. C.-L. (2019). Plant-Based Diets Are Associated With a Lower Risk of Incident Cardiovascular Disease, Cardiovascular Disease Mortality, and All-Cause Mortality in a General Population of Middle-Aged Adults. *Journal of the American Heart Association*, https://www.ahajournals.org/doi/epub/10.1161/JAHA.119.012865.

Koenig, H. G. (2012, December 16). *Religion, Spirituality, and Health: The Research and Clinical Implications.* Retrieved from National Library of Medicine: https://www.ncbi.nlm.nih.gov/pmc/articles/PMC3671693/?utm

_source=link_newsv9&utm_campaign=item_389510&utm_medium=copy

Lyubomirsky, S. (2009, July 14). *What If I'd Never Met My Husband.* Retrieved from Scientific American: https://www.scientificamerican.com/article/what-if-id-never-husband/

Lyubomirsky, S. S. (2005). Pursuing Happiness: The Architecture of Sustainable Change. *Review of General Psychology*, pp. 111–131.

McGonigal, J. (2012, June). *The game that can give you 10 extra years of life.* Retrieved from https://www.ted.com: https://www.ted.com/talks/jane_mcgonigal_the_game_that_can_give_you_10_extra_years_of_life?language=en

Merriam-Webster Dictionary. (2023, March 4). *compassion noun.* Retrieved from https://www.merriam-webster.com/dictionary: https://www.merriam-webster.com/dictionary/compassion

Milson, J. (n.d.). *"Judge Softly" or "Walk a Mile in His Moccasins" — by Mary T. Lathrap.* Retrieved from https://jamesmilson.com/: https://jamesmilson.com/about-the-blog/judge-softly-or-walk-a-mile-in-his-moccasins-by-mary-t-lathrap/

Mosing, M. A., Zietsch, B. P., Shekar, S. N., Wright, M. J., & Martin, N. G. (2009, July 18). Genetic and Environmental Influences on Optimism and its Relationship to Mental and Self-Rated Health:A Study of Aging Twins. *Springer Science+Business Media*, pp. 1-8.

New World Encyclopedia . (2022, November 24). *Personality assessment.* Retrieved from https://www.newworldencyclopedia.org/:

https://www.newworldencyclopedia.org/entry/Personality_assessment

Newport PhD, F. (2022, February 4). *Religion and Wellbeing in the U.S.: Update.* Retrieved from Gallup News: https://news.gallup.com/opinion/polling-matters/389510/religion-wellbeing-update.aspx

Odgers, C. L. (2020, March). Annual Research Review: Adolescent mental health in the digital age: facts, fears, and future directions. *Journal of Child Psychology and Psychiatry*, pp. 336-348.

Office of Disease Prevention and Health Promotion. (2023). *The Physical Activity Guidelines for Americans.* Retrieved from health.gov: https://health.gov/our-work/nutrition-physical-activity/physical-activity-guidelines/current-guidelines

Pathak, V., Jena, B., & Kalra, S. (2013, July-September). *Perspectives in Clinical Research: Qualitative research.* Retrieved from National Library of Medicine: https://www.ncbi.nlm.nih.gov/pmc/articles/PMC3757586/

Pearce M, G. L. (2022). Association Between Physical Activity and Risk of Depression: A Systematic Review and Meta-analysis. *JAMA Psychiatry*, 550-559.

Peterson, C. a. (2014). Meaning and Positive Psychology. *International Journal of Existential Psychology & Psychotherapy*, 1-7.

Powell, A. (2012, February 2). *Decoding keys to a healthy life: 74 years young, Harvard study continues to yield a treasure trove of data.* Retrieved from http://news.harvard.edu/: http://news.harvard.edu/gazette/story/2012/02/decoding-keys-to-a-healthy-life/

Pursuit of Happiness. (2023). *Barbara Fredrickson.* Retrieved from Pursuit of Happiness: https://www.pursuit-of-happiness.org/history-of-happiness/barb-fredrickson/

Ray, J. (2021, July 20). *2020 Sets Records for Negative Emotions.* Retrieved from news.gallup.com: https://news.gallup.com/poll/352205/2020-sets-records-negative-emotions.aspx

Regan, A., Walsh, L. C., & Lyubomirsky, S. (2022, October 2). Are Some Ways of Expressing Gratitude More Benefcial Than Others? *Affective Science*, pp. 1-10.

Rippstein-Leuenberger, K., Mauthner, O., Sexton, J. B., & Schwendimann, R. (2017, June 13). A qualitative analysis of the Three Good Things intervention in healthcare workers. *BMJ Open*, pp. 1-6.

Roden, B. (n.d.). *5 Famous Literary Quotes Explained: "Two roads diverged in a wood, and I—I took the one less traveled by".* Retrieved from https://www.historythroughfiction.com/: https://www.historythroughfiction.com/blog/famous-literary-quotes-five#:~:text=This%20line%20comes%20from%20a,a%20means%20of%20celebrating%20individualism.

Sears, L. E. (2013). Overall well-being as a predictor of health care, productivity, and retention outcomes in a large employer. *Population health management*, 397–405.

Seligman, M. (2010). Flourish: Positive Psychology. *The Tanner Lectures on Human Values*, (pp. 1-56). Michigan.

Seligman, M. (2011). *Flourish: A Visionary New Understanding of Happiness and Well-Being.* New York: Simon & Schuster, Inc.

Seligman, M. (2013). *Flourish.* New York: Simon & Schuster.

Shenk, J. (2009, June). What Makes Us Happy? *The Atlantic.* Retrieved from http://www.theatlantic.com/: http://www.theatlantic.com/magazine/archive/2009/06/what-makes-us-happy/307439/

Smithsonian Institution. (2022, July 11). *Introduction to Human Evolution.* Retrieved from https://humanorigins.si.edu/: https://humanorigins.si.edu/education/introduction-human-evolution#:~:text=Scientific%20evidence%20shows%20that%20the,of%20approximately%20six%20million%20years.

Srivastava, T. (2016, February 18). *THE ESSENCE OF EDUCATION.* Retrieved from http://www.pioneershiksha.com/: http://www.pioneershiksha.com/news/3073-the-essence-of-education.html#:~:text=Education%20is%20the%20only%20key,ends%20when%20our%20life%20ends.

Tech & Science Dictionary. (2023). *meta-analysis.* Retrieved from https://www.dictionary.com/: https://www.dictionary.com/e/tech-science/meta-analysis/#:~:text=What%20does%20meta%2Danalysis%20mean,and%20to%20identify%20overall%20trends.

ThePirateKing777. (n.d.). *Eternal Transcendence.* https://powerlisting.fandom.com/wiki/Eternal_Transcendence.

Thomas, L. (2022, October 24). *Longitudinal Study | Definition, Approaches & Examples.* Retrieved from https://www.scribbr.com: https://www.scribbr.com/methodology/longitudinal-study/

U.S. Bureau of Labor Statistics. (2022, February 9). *7.8 million workers had an illness-related work absence in January*

*2022*. Retrieved from https://www.bls.gov/: https://www.bls.gov/opub/ted/2022/7-8-million-workers-had-an-illness-related-work-absence-in-january-2022.htm

Vaish, A. G. (2008). Not all emotions are created equal: the negativity bias in social-emotional development. *Psychological Bulletin*, pp. 383–403.

Wehrwein, P. (2011, October 20). *Astounding increase in antidepressant use by Americans.* Retrieved from https://www.health.harvard.edu/: https://www.health.harvard.edu/blog/astounding-increase-in-antidepressant-use-by-americans-201110203624

World Population Review. (2023). *Divorce Rate by State 2023.* Retrieved from https://worldpopulationreview.com/: https://worldpopulationreview.com/state-rankings/divorce-rate-by-state

Made in the USA
Columbia, SC
01 September 2024

41380638R00076